# Celebrate THE Century™

## A COLLECTION OF COMMEMORATIVE STAMPS

*1960-1969*

## UNITED STATES POSTAL SERVICE

POSTMASTER GENERAL
AND CHIEF EXECUTIVE OFFICER
*William J. Henderson*

CHIEF MARKETING OFFICER
*Allen Kane*

EXECUTIVE DIRECTOR, STAMP SERVICES
*Azeezaly S. Jaffer*

MANAGER, STAMP MARKETING
*Gary A. Thuro*

PROJECT MANAGER
*Clarence R. Williams*

TIME-LIFE BOOKS IS A DIVISION OF TIME LIFE INC.

### TIME-LIFE
### CUSTOM PUBLISHING

VICE PRESIDENT AND PUBLISHER
*Neil Levin*

DIRECTOR OF NEW PRODUCT DEVELOPMENT
*Teresa Graham*

PROJECT COORDINATOR
*Jennifer L. Ward*

PRINTING PRODUCTION MANAGER
*Vanessa Hunnibell*

### EDITORIAL STAFF FOR
### CELEBRATE THE CENTURY

MANAGING EDITOR
*Morin Bishop*

EDITORS
*John Bolster, Sarah Brash*

DESIGNERS
*Barbara Chilenskas, Jia Baek*

WRITER/RESEARCHERS
*Ward Calhoun, Theresa Deal,
Rachael Nevins, Ylann Schemm*

PHOTO EDITOR
*Bill Broyles*

First printing. Printed in U.S.A.

TIME-LIFE is a trademark of Time Warner Inc. U.S.A.

LIBRARY OF CONGRESS CATALOGING-IN-PUBLICATION DATA
Celebrate the century: a collection of commemorative stamps.
p. cm.    Includes index.
Contents: v. 7. 1960–1969
ISBN 0-7835-5323-4
1. Commemorative postage stamps—United States—History—20th century.
2. United States—History—20th century.
I. Time-Life Books

HE6185.U5C45  1998                                97–46952
769.56973—DC21                                   CIP

Books produced by Time-Life Custom Publishing are available at a special bulk discount for promotional and premium use. Custom adaptations can also be created to meet your specific marketing goals. Call 1-800-323-5255.

## PICTURE CREDITS

Cover, Corbis-Bettmann; 4, P.J. Griffiths; 5, UPI/Corbis-Bettmann; 6, Ernest Sisto/*New York Times*/Archive Photos; 7, Bob Henriques/Magnum; 8, Tom Miner/Image Works; 9, Johnson Space Center/NASA; 10, Archive Photos; 11, UPI/Corbis-Bettmann; 12, Charles Moore/Black Star; 13, top, Charles Moore/Black Star; bottom, Bob Adelman/Magnum; 14, UPI/Corbis-Bettmann; 15, top, Leonard Freed/Magnum; bottom, UPI/Corbis-Bettmann; 16, UPI/Corbis-Bettmann; 17, top, Movie Still Archives; stamp, Ford® and Mustang® are registered trademarks of the Ford Motor Co.; 18, both, Ford Motor Company; 19, top, UPI/Corbis-Bettmann; bottom, AP/Wide World Photos; 20, left, Ford Motor Company; right, UPI/Corbis-Bettmann; 21, Ford Motor Company; 22, Neil Leifer/*Sports Illustrated*; 23, Vernon J. Biever; 24, left, NFL Photos; right, Walter Iooss Jr./*Sports Illustrated*; 25, Vernon J. Biever; 26, Neil Leifer/*Sports Illustrated*; 27, both, Walter Iooss Jr.; 28, Robert Freeman/Apple; 29, top, Corbis-Bettmann; stamp, "The Beatles" Apple Corps Limited, "Yellow Submarine" Subafilms Limited; 30, top, Charles Trainor, inset, UPI/Corbis-Bettmann, bottom, UPI/Corbis-Bettmann; 31, Robert Freeman/© Apple Corps Ltd; 32, *Hard Day's Night* still, Culver Pictures; 33, top Ethan Russell/Apple, bottom, Harry Benson/Hulton Getty/Liaison; 34, Wayne Miller/Magnum; 35, all, Fairchild Communications; 36, Archive Photos; 37, all, Texas Instruments; 38, UPI/Corbis-Bettmann; 39, UPI/Corbis-Bettmann; 40, P.J. Griffiths/Magnum; 41, top, Corbis-Bettmann; bottom, Superstock; 42, UPI/Corbis-Bettmann; 43, top, UPI/Corbis-Bettmann; inset, UPI/Corbis-Bettmann; bottom, Underwood Photo Archives, SF; 44, Hallmark; 45, left, Mattel; center and right, David Levinthal; stamp, Barbie and associated trademarks are owned by Mattel, Inc.© 1999 Mattel, Inc. All Rights Reserved. Used with permission; 46, both, Mattel; 47, top, Archive Photos; inset, Mattel; 48, left, Mattel; center, Sarah Eames; right, David Levinthal; 49, top right, Allan Grant; center, Sarah Eames; bottom left, David Levinthal; bottom right, David Levinthal; 50, Rowland Scherman/Black Star; 51, top, JFK Library; stamp, The Peace Corps in Ethiopia © 1966 The Norman Rockwell Family Trust; 52, Paul Conklin/Peace Corps; 53, top right, Paul Conklin/Peace Corps; center, Joan Larson/Peace Corps; bottom right, Paul Conklin/Peace Corps; 54, top, Rowland Scherman/Black Star; bottom, Paul Conklin/Peace Corps; 55, Paul Conklin/Peace Corps; 56, UPI/Corbis-Bettmann; 57, top, UPI/Corbis-Bettmann; stamp, © Roger Maris Family. Made under license with Mrs. Roger Maris. Major League Baseball trademarks and copyrights are used with permission of Major League Baseball Properties, Inc.; 58, UPI/Corbis-Bettmann; 59, top left, Transcendental Graphics; inset, UPI/Corbis-Bettmann; bottom right, UPI/Corbis-Bettmann; 60, left, UPI/Corbis-Bettmann; 60-61, UPI/Corbis-Bettmann; 61, right, UPI/Corbis-Bettmann; 62, Shelley Rusten/Black Star; 63, top, Elliot Landy/Magnum; stamp, Woodstock and the guitar-and-dove logo are registered trademarks of Woodstock Ventures LC; 64, top left, Hulton Getty/Liaison; bottom right, Photofest; 64-65, Photofest; 65, top right, Collection of Charles Heigl Michelet; center right, Associated Press; bottom left, Archive Photos; 66, top, Shelley Rustin/Black Star; bottom, Henry Diltz/Image Works; 67, top, Allan Koss/Image Works; bottom, left to right, Archive Photos (2), Shelley Rustin/Black Star, Elliot Landy/Magnum; 68, Johnson Sace Center/NASA; 69, Johnson Space Center/NASA; 70, Kennedy Space Center/NASA; 71, all, Johnson Space Center/NASA; 72, both, Johnson Space Center/NASA; 73, Johnson Space Center/NASA; 74, Globe Photos; 75, Fred Ward/Black Star; 76, AP/Wide World Photos; 77, top, AP/Wide World Photos; bottom, Dennis Brack/Black Star; 78, top, Black Star; bottom left, UPI/Corbis-Bettmann; bottom right, Underwood Photo Archives SF; 79, left, UPI/Corbis-Bettmann; inset, Archive Photos; 80, Archive Photos; 81, top, Globe Photos; stamp, *STAR TREK™* & © 1999 Paramount Pictures. All Rights Reserved.; 82, top left, Globe Photos; top right, Globe Photos; center, Movie Still Archives; 83, Archive Photos; 84, left, Globe Photos; right, Movie Still Archives; inset, Globe Photos; 85, top, Globe Photos; inset, Jet Propulsion Lab/NASA; 86, Walter Iooss Jr.; 87, Walter Iooss Jr; 88, left, Walter Iooss Jr.; 88-89, Neil Leifer; 90, Vernon J. Biever; 91, UPI/Corbis-Bettmann; 92, Archive Photos; 93, Archive Photos; 94, left, HRL Labs; right, AP/Wide World Photos; 95, left, Jonathan Blair/Corbis; right, Photofest.

# CONTENTS

American involvement in Vietnam (opposite page) produced dissension and conflict at home (above).

# INTRODUCTION

In January 1960, Arthur Schlesinger Jr. looked into his historian's crystal ball and described what Americans might expect of the new decade: "The Sixties," he wrote, "will probably be spirited, articulate, inventive, incoherent, turbulent, with energy shooting off wildly in all directions." Looking back from the perspective of the late 1990s, Schlesinger's prognostication seems remarkably apt, even though it only hints at the social and political divisions—over everything from hair length to the war in Vietnam—that would polarize Americans to a degree not seen since the Civil War. And no one could have foreseen how dramatically the nation would be transformed, both for better and for worse.

When the decade opened, Americans, especially the members of the burgeoning middle class, looked toward the future with a large measure of optimism, for they were continuing to enjoy the extraordinary economic boom that began when World War II ended and showed no signs of letting up. Unemployment dipped to as low as 3.5 percent, and between 1960 and 1969 per capita income jumped by 41 percent. Since prices were fairly stable during the decade, the hike in income made a significant difference in the average family's lifestyle. Americans spent their money on big-ticket items like a house in the suburbs (or a trade-up from a modest Levittown-style home to a larger, more expensive one) or two cars in the garage. One sign of how flush the times were is the fact that in the first four months after Ford introduced its latest model, the Mustang, more than 100,000 people indulged themselves in the sporty new car. Fatter paychecks also translated into what had once been luxuries but now seemed like necessities: television sets (93 percent of American households had at least one in the '60s); baseball gear for juvenile Mickey Mantle wannabes; Barbie® dolls, with ever-expanding wardrobes and a plethora of accessories, for the girls in the family; and a stereo and the latest Beatles album for the teenagers.

And there were children aplenty to shower with material pleasures. The baby boom that started when the soldiers came home in 1945 didn't end until 1964, and by that time the oldest of the boomers were reaching college age. In this golden age of prosperity, more and more middle-class families could afford to send their children to college, and enrollment swelled to historic highs across the country.

The man elected president in 1960 seemed well suited to lead a nation with so large a proportion of young people, most of whom who were just as optimistic about the future as their elders. Vigorous, attractive, youthful—at 43, he was the youngest man ever elected to the office—John Fitzgerald Kennedy declared at his inauguration, "Let the word go forth, from this time and place, to friend and foe alike, that the torch has been passed to a new generation of Americans." He went on to issue his famous challenge to turn idealism into action: "Ask not what your country can do for you; ask what you can do for your country.... Ask not what America will do for you, but what together we can do for the freedom of man."

**Roger Maris transfixed the nation with his pursuit of Babe Ruth's home run record.**

Less than two months after he took office, Kennedy announced the formation of the Peace Corps as a way for energetic idealists to put their principles into action in underdeveloped countries. Tens of thousands of young people applied to the program, and even those who didn't step forward to volunteer were excited by the idea of service. Besides providing technical aid and education, the volunteers were unofficial ambassadors for American democracy. The hope was that their influence would make communism less appealing to the people they worked with.

The tension between the U.S.S.R. and the United States was at a high point in the early years of the decade, and one of President Kennedy's most pressing concerns was Cuba. In 1959 Fidel Castro had overthrown a pro-American dictatorship and established a Communist reign only 90 miles from the United States. Castro's close relations with the Soviet Union sparked the most terrifying episode of the Cold War. On October 22, 1962, President Kennedy revealed to the nation that a U.S. spy plane flying over Cuba had spotted missile bases set up by the Soviet Union.

Some of the missiles already in place were armed with nuclear warheads and were capable of striking U.S. cities as far north as Washington, D.C. For six agonizing days the world held its breath while the president and Russian premier Nikita Khrushchev exchanged threats before finally defusing the crisis. Promising not to invade Cuba as it had threatened, the U.S. would dismantle its own missile bases in Turkey, which posed a threat to the Soviet Union. For their part, the Soviets would remove their missiles from Cuba. In the four decades of the Cold War, the Cuban missile crisis was the closest the world ever came to a nuclear confrontation.

On the domestic front, the major issue during the Kennedy years was the struggle for racial equality. The Jim Crow laws on the books in southern states made blacks second-class citizens, denying them, among other things, access to public accommodations. Beginning in 1960, at the urging of inspirational leaders like Martin Luther King, black college students staged hundreds of sit-ins at white-only lunch counters, and as a result a number of cities did away with some forms of discrimination. But what was really needed was a display of federal muscle. In 1963 President Kennedy proposed a civil rights bill, but it remained unfinished business when he was assassinated on November 22 of that year.

It fell to a southerner, President Lyndon Johnson, to shepherd—or bully—a sweeping civil rights bill through Congress in 1964. It forbade racial discrimination in hotels and other businesses catering to the public and empowered the Justice Department to move against segregation in schools, hospitals and other public institutions. The bill also proscribed discrimination in employment on the basis of race, color, religion, national origin and sex.

Keeping up the momentum, President Johnson wrangled another civil rights bill through Congress the next year. The 1965 Voting Rights

**The stirring rhetoric and herculean efforts of Martin Luther King helped produce landmark civil rights legislation in the '60s.**

Act guaranteed that federal registrars would be sent to the South to support black citizens attempting to register and vote. The act was destined to have a tremendous impact. Within three years, the percentage of eligible blacks in the South who were registered voters would rise to 60 percent, the same as the rate for white southerners.

But legislation could erase only some of the evils of racism, and that became tragically clear just five days after the president signed the Voting Rights Act into law on August 6. In Los Angeles' largest black ghetto, Watts, a seemingly minor incident—a young man's arrest for drunk driving—touched off a riot after his mother scuffled with the police. When the burning, looting and shooting ended five days later, 34 people were dead, some 900 had been injured, 4,000 had been arrested and 200 businesses had been reduced to ashes. The nation was aghast at the violence it had witnessed on television.

Even before Watts there had been several smaller disturbances in black urban neighborhoods outside the South. But the sheer magni-

**The music festival at Woodstock gave young Americans an opportunity to celebrate the counterculture.**

tude of Watts sent the nation an ominous, unmistakable message about the anger and despair that had taken root among blacks living in the North, West and Midwest. Theoretically, blacks outside the South enjoyed the same civil rights as whites, but being able to vote did little to ameliorate economic inequity and deep-rooted racism. Nationwide, both the poverty rate and the unemployment rate were about two and a half times higher for nonwhites than for whites. These conditions fueled a growing militancy, especially among younger blacks. They dismissed civil rights leaders like Martin Luther King as Uncle Toms kowtowing to the white power structure and embraced "black power" as their rallying cry.

Riots ripped through America's ghettos during the summers of 1966 and 1967. But the most tragic of all the uprisings followed King's assassination by a white drifter in Memphis in 1968. More than 100 cities were rocked by violence that left 39 people dead. Worst hit was the nation's capital, where hundreds of blazing fires made

the city look as though it had been fire-bombed.

The unifying middle ground of the civil rights movement that King had labored so valiantly to create eroded. President Johnson did get one more civil rights bill through Congress outlawing racial discrimination in housing. But for the rest of the decade, progress was hamstrung by a powerful white backlash.

Nineteen-sixty-eight turned out to be a year of relentless turmoil and conflict. While President Johnson was fighting the good fight for racial justice, launching the Medicare and Medicaid programs, and liberalizing immigration policy, he was self-destructing as a politician. The problem was Vietnam, which was turning out to be the longest war in U.S. history—and, by 1968, the most unpopular. American involvement in the war between anti-Communist, Western-dominated South Vietnam and the Communist and fiercely nationalist North had been fairly limited until 1965, when Johnson sent the first combat troops to Vietnam and started a bombing campaign against the North.

8

Over the next few years the war escalated relentlessly, and so did the antiwar movement. Many in the movement's vanguard were college students who were opposed to the draft or thought that the U.S. had improperly injected itself into a divided country's civil war. The future of Vietnam, they believed, must be determined by its people and not by a foreign power.

Many older, more conservative citizens denounced the youthful protesters as anti-American; the young people retorted that no one over 30 should be trusted. This "generation gap" only became wider and more bitter as the war dragged on.

Nevertheless, many middle-of-the-road Americans were having qualms about the war, and those qualms turned to outright opposition when Communist forces staged a powerful surprise offensive in early 1968. Only recently the government had declared that the war was going well and that there was "light at the end of the tunnel," but after the Tet offensive many citizens believed they had been lied to. President Johnson's approval rating plummeted, and he announced that he would not seek reelection.

More shocks were to come. While campaigning for the Democratic presidential nomination, Robert Kennedy was gunned down in a Los Angeles hotel. The Democratic convention in Chicago was the scene of a week-long violent confrontation between the police and 10,000 young demonstrators, most of whom came to voice their antiwar sentiments. The Democratic candidate, Hubert Humphrey, was hopelessly compromised by the bloodletting, and Republican Richard Nixon emerged victorious in November.

Although riven by political and social discord,

**More than any other event, Buzz Aldrin's walk on the Moon brought a divided America together.**

Americans were united on the night of July 20, 1969, by the thrilling spectacle of Apollo 11 astronauts Buzz Aldrin and Neil Armstrong walking and cavorting like spacesuited kangaroos on the Moon. It was President Kennedy who had boldly committed the nation to putting a man on the Moon (and returning him safely) by the end of the decade. His audacity had a fantastic payoff, for the lunar landing was the greatest technological achievement and the greatest human adventure of all time. Technology and science had seen amazing advances in the 1960s, including the laser, the integrated circuit, and the first successful heart transplant. But nothing approached the magnitude of Apollo 11. The week of the Moon shot was, President Nixon exulted, "the greatest week in the history of the world since Creation."

# "I HAVE A DREAM"

More than 35 years after its triumphant final strains reverberated off the historic monuments and government buildings in our nation's capital, Martin Luther King Jr.'s "I Have a Dream" speech has lost none of its power. Captured on film, the majestic oration is one of the most memorable speeches of all time, and a landmark in U.S. history. So much so that, simply reading a copy of the text, one can't help but hear King's resonant baritone in the mind: "…America has given the Negro people a bad check which has come back marked 'insufficient funds.' But we refuse to believe that the bank of justice is bankrupt."

King's audience on that steamy August afternoon in 1963 stretched along the reflecting pool in Washington, D.C., between the Lincoln Memorial, where King stood, and the Washington Monument, half a mile away. Numbering close to 250,000, they had come to march on Washington as the culmination of a summer of protest, conflict and bloodshed that had riveted the world's attention on black Americans' struggle for basic human rights.

That struggle, centuries old, caught fire in 1955 when a woman named Rosa Parks, tired at the end of a workday, refused to give up her seat to a white passenger and move to the back of a Montgomery, Alabama, bus as required by city law. Parks was arrested, and local black residents, rallying to support her, launched a boycott of city buses. They chose King, the new pastor of Montgomery's Dexter Avenue Baptist Church, to spearhead the cause. A son of Atlanta with a Ph.D. in theology from Boston University, King gained national recognition as a powerful speaker and charismatic leader for his role in Montgomery. Despite being jailed and having his house bombed, he saw the boycott through to a successful conclusion: In November

**With the Washington Monument in the background (left), King (above) made his stirring appeal to the nation's conscience.**

*The name, likeness, signature and copyrighted words of Dr. Martin Luther King Jr. are used by permission of Intellectual Properties Management, Atlanta, Georgia, as exclusive licensor of the King Estate.*

1956, the Supreme Court ruled that Alabama's laws mandating segregation in public transportation were unconstitutional.

The following year King helped found the Southern Christian Leadership Conference (SCLC) and opened the struggle on a wider front. Having studied and admired the nonviolent protest tactics of Mohandas Gandhi, King put them to use in the civil rights movement. He traveled to India in 1959 to learn more about Gandhi's legacy.

As the '60s dawned, other activist groups sprang to action in the South. The Student Nonviolent Coordinating Committee (SNCC) organized sit-ins in segregated restaurants. The Congress of Racial Equality (CORE) initiated "Freedom Rides," a campaign to integrate interstate bus travel in the South that resulted in scores of violent conflicts. King moved to Atlanta to focus on his duties as president of the SCLC. Within two months of the first sit-in, activists in 54 cities in nine states had held sit-ins of their own.

The movement reached a climax in the spring of '63 when King and the SCLC brought protesters to Birmingham, Alabama, the state's largest—and most rigidly segregated—city. Notorious for its bigoted police officers and their intransigent commander, Bull Connor, Birmingham roiled with demonstrations and brutal police crackdowns for most of the spring. Images of Connor and his men turning attack dogs and high-powered fire hoses on the protesters were broadcast around the world. King's crusaders

The police dogs (left) and fire hoses (above) demonstrators faced in Birmingham shocked Americans into recognizing the need for justice that King so eloquently expressed in his oratory in Washington (right).

prevailed, and in June President John F. Kennedy responded to Birmingham by submitting broad civil rights legislation to Congress. Demonstrations continued nationwide all summer and on August 28, as federal lawmakers debated the Civil Rights Act, the March on Washington unified the movement.

Introduced by civil rights pioneer A. Philip Randolph as "the moral leader of the nation," King was the final speaker of the long hot afternoon. The marchers were restless, and pockets of them had drifted off when he stepped to the podium in front of the Lincoln Memorial. Echoing the language of Lincoln's Gettysburg Address in his opening, King soon had the massive gathering riveted to his every eloquent phrase. The promise of the Emancipation Proclamation, he explained, had not been upheld in the intervening 100 years. Despite the difficulties and frustrations that African Americans faced, King continued, his voice rising in passion and determination, he still had a dream: "It is a dream deeply rooted in the American dream. I have a dream that one day this nation will rise up and live out the true

14

King's de facto leadership of the civil rights movement was evident in his prominent place among the marchers on Washington (left), his presence behind Johnson at the signing of the 1964 Civil Rights Act (below) and in the adulation of the crowds who constantly thronged around him (right).

# Aftermath

President Kennedy was assassinated three months after the March on Washington, but his successor, Lyndon Johnson, ushered the Civil Rights Act into law on July 2, 1964. King was named *Time* magazine's Man of the Year for 1963 and won the 1964 Nobel Peace Prize.

He continued to crusade for equality and became black America's foremost leader, despite challenges from the more militant Malcolm X, and despite his countless enemies, including FBI chief J. Edgar Hoover. On April 4, 1968, while visiting Memphis to support striking sanitation workers, King was gunned down by an assassin as he stood on the balcony outside his hotel room. James Earl Ray later pleaded guilty to the crime.

On November 2, 1983, President Ronald Reagan signed a bill establishing a federal holiday in honor of Martin Luther King Jr., which was first observed in January 1986.

meaning of its creed: 'We hold these truths to be self-evident: that all men are created equal.' "

Shouts came back to him from the audience now. As he approached his awesome crescendo, King quoted "America (My Country, 'Tis of Thee)," saying that when his dream of equality came true, America could let freedom ring across the land and "speed up the day when all of God's children ... will be able to join hands and sing in the words of the old Negro spiritual, 'Free at last! Free at last! Thank God Almighty, we are free at last!' "

# FORD MUSTANG

Racing legend A. J. Foyt may have taken the checkered flag at the 1964 Indianapolis 500, but the brightest star at the speedway that year was the Official Pace Car, Ford's dazzling new white Mustang. Ford produced dozens of Mustangs, including 37 convertibles, for the Memorial Day weekend festivities at Indy, and the sporty new cars wowed the thousands of fans in the grandstands as well as the millions watching at home. Foyt probably didn't mind being upstaged by the Mustang—he got to take one home with him.

More than 100,000 people took Mustangs home in the first four months of the car's availability. The ponycar, as it was promptly nicknamed, came in a rainbow of colors—Pagoda Green, Caspian Blue, Silversmoke Gray and Rangoon Red, among others—and its clean, vigorous lines broke new ground in automotive design. The car also broke the record for first-

year sales of a new model: 418,000 Mustangs were trotted out of dealerships by April 1965. One year later that figure topped one million. Ford had the most popular new car ever on its hands, but, as attractive as the Mustang was, it didn't quite sell itself.

Well before the Indy 500, Ford launched an unprecedented stampede of publicity for the Mustang. Coordinated by the Ford division's whiz-kid general manager, Lee Iacocca, and executed by the ad agency J. Walter Thompson, the Mustang promotional blitz started with ubiquitous print, radio and TV ads. Iacocca orchestrated April cover stories on the Mustang in *Time* and *Newsweek*. Ford even ran ads for its ads. Newspaper spots boldly declared that "The Most Exciting Thing on TV Tonight Will Be a Commercial" and urged viewers to tune in to prime time that night to catch a glimpse of "the year's most exciting new car." On April 17, the

**Henry Ford II unveiled the Mustang at the 1964 World's Fair (left); its image was enhanced by a starring role in *Bullitt* (above).**

"It's a fun, beautiful, *sexy* car. It makes the passengers feel happy and sexy."

—*J. Orion Bunk,
owner of Beverly Hills
Mustang, 1984*

18

The Mustang GT's nimble handling was developed through heavy testing (opposite, above); Mustang's role as pace car at the Indy 500 provided it with invaluable exposure (opposite, inset); in 1963 Ford developed the prototype Mustang II (above), but the car was never mass-produced; the original Mustang (top) was billed as both sporty—particularly in the convertible model—and inexpensive.

day the car went on sale, the Mustang was unveiled at the World's Fair in New York. Twenty-two thousand orders poured into Ford dealerships that day.

Clearly, the time was right for the Mustang. Up to that point, American sports cars had been two-seaters, such as the Chevrolet Corvette, that were patterned after European models and invariably priced out of the average car buyer's range. Four-seaters were typically huge gas-guzzlers that seemed designed by—and intended for—your grandfather. Ford recognized that the largest segment of the population, baby boomers, were just beginning to come of age and shrewdly realized that though young people might not have money to burn, they would appreciate an affordable, snappy-looking "personal" car. The company's goal was to bring the Mustang to the street with a base price under

The Mustang offered a Select Shift (above), which allowed drivers to operate the vehicle in manual or automatic mode and allegedly ensured domestic tranquillity; Shelby (right) created the high-performance Shelby GT-350; one Mustang ad campaign (opposite) included a fanciful Mustang pledge.

$3,000. To keep costs down, the Mustang would borrow several structural elements from the Ford Falcon, but ultimately, the slick Mustang and the boxy Falcon had about as much in common as their counterparts in nature.

Eugene Bordinat, Ford's director of styling, designed the first prototype, Mustang I, in 1962. A two-seater with a race-car look, the Mustang I was sleeker than the final product, but its design greatly influenced that of later models. The Mustang II appeared the following year. This prototype looked more like a conventional car than the Mustang I, and it gave way in 1964 to the four-seater production Mustang, the beauty that won the 1964 Tiffany Gold Medal Award for Excellence in Design; it was the first time the award had gone to an automobile design.

With Mustangs galloping off showroom floors, Ford hardly needed to tinker with a good thing. Yet the company did modify the car, to remarkably favorable effect. For the model year

# Aftermath

With the millennium fast approaching, the Mustang legend continues at a steady canter. The 1999 model is as racy and sporty as any, and 1960s-era ponycars, which have enjoyed several rebirths in popularity, have lost none of their élan. In the 1980s Beverly Hills had its own classic Mustang dealership, and celebrities such as Richard Gere, Alan Alda and Ringo Starr have been known to request vintage Mustangs whenever they rent from the Hollywood Rent-A-Wreck, which has a stable of classic Mustangs.

Ford's slogan for the restyled 30th anniversary 1994 Mustang touted, "It is what it was. And more." *Motor Trend* named the '94 Mustang Car of the Year. Ford plans another significant redesign for the year 2000.

1965, Ford introduced a fastback Mustang, as handsome as its coupe and convertible cousins, and even sportier. Ford also teamed up with race-car builder Carroll Shelby, who left his imprint on the brand with his Shelby-American Mustang Cobras. His limited edition Shelby GT-350 fastback, a muscular racer, became an instant legend upon its debut in 1965.

The Mustang image was further burnished by the 1968 film *Bullitt*, which featured Steve McQueen careening over the hills of San Francisco in a '67 model. McQueen did all the driving himself, and the sequence remains one of the most famous movie chase scenes of all time.

In the model year 1969 Ford significantly redesigned the ponycar, giving it a more rounded look, a deeper grille cavity and eliminating its side indentation. That year also saw the introduction of the Mach I, Grande and Boss Mustangs. Ford would restyle the Mustang once more, in the '70s, before the age of the classic Mustang drew to a close in 1973.

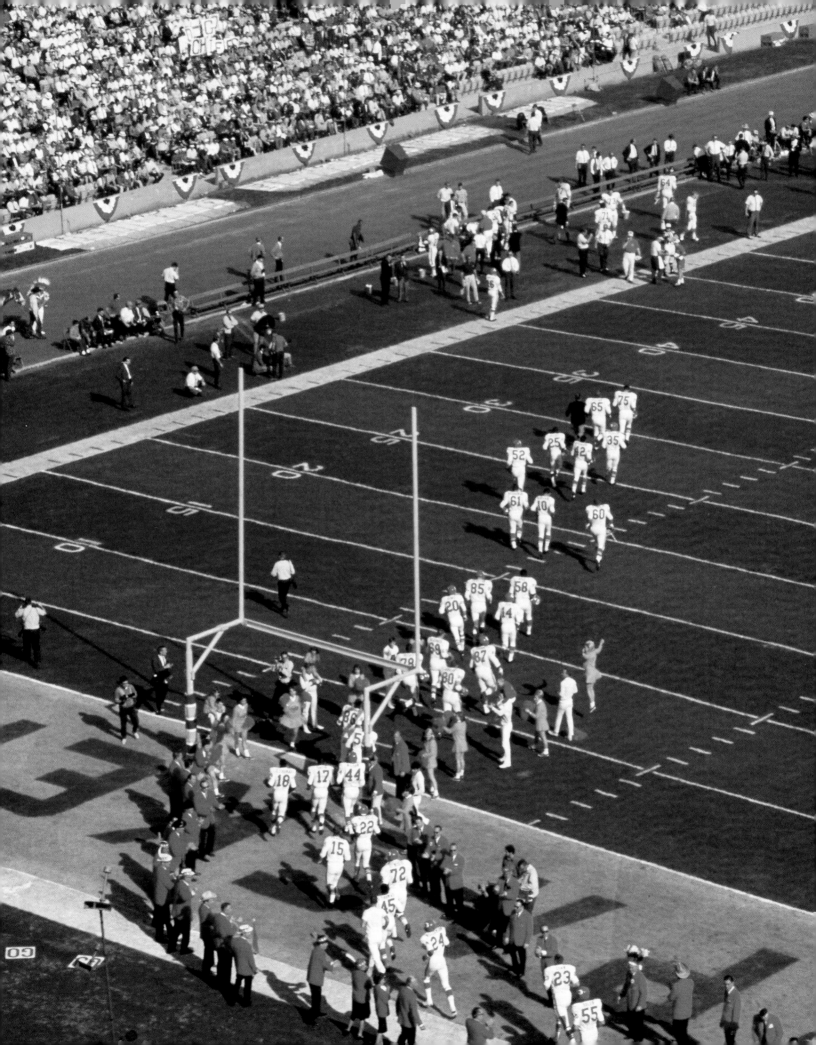

# SUPER BOWL I

Crashing a party is a difficult proposition. As an uninvited guest, you are rarely welcome, and if you do make it in, chances are you won't find any friends and you'll leave early. So it was no small feat when the upstart American Football League crashed a long-running National Football League engagement and stuck around to help create pro football's greatest party, the Super Bowl.

The AFL, which began play in 1960, was formed by Texan Lamar Hunt, who decided to form a league to rival the NFL after his unsuccessful bid in 1958 to purchase the NFL's Chicago Cardinals franchise. Hunt's partners in the venture included entrepreneurs Bud Adams in Houston, Ralph Wilson in Buffalo and Oakland's Y. C. Soda. Although the original eight AFL teams were comprised mainly of NFL castoffs, they began competing almost immediately with the more established league for prize college recruits.

Louisiana State running back Billy Cannon won the 1959 Heisman Trophy and was signed to an NFL contract by then-Los Angeles Rams general manager Pete Rozelle after the regular season—but before that year's Sugar Bowl. Adams of the AFL's Houston Oilers signed him after the bowl game, and a judge later ruled in favor of the Oilers' contract because the Rams had violated NCAA rules by signing Cannon before the completion of his season. The battle between the two leagues had begun in earnest.

In 1965 the AFL signed a five-year, $36-million TV contract with NBC, thus giving it the necessary funds and exposure to compete with the NFL on an equal footing. That stability, combined with the vast sums both leagues were now spending in their bidding wars over top college talent and, eventually, over one another's star players, convinced owners in both leagues that the idea of uniting the two leagues

**Chiefs' coach Hank Stram, Rozelle and Hunt (above, left to right) helped make the first Super Bowl (left) possible.**

"We've just beaten Dallas for our second straight championship. But if we lose this game, people will remember us as the NFL team that lost to Kansas City in the first game played between the [two] leagues."

—*TOM BROWN, Green Bay safety, January 1967*

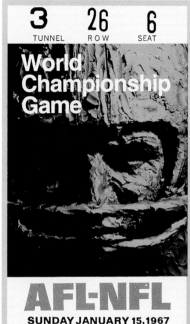

The first Super Bowl ticket billed the event as the AFL-NFL World Championship Game (above)—it would not be "Super" until 1969; while McGee (right) was easing the pain of a hangover with a seven-catch day, Kansas City quarterback Len Dawson (opposite) was suffering the headache of coping with Green Bay's stifling defense.

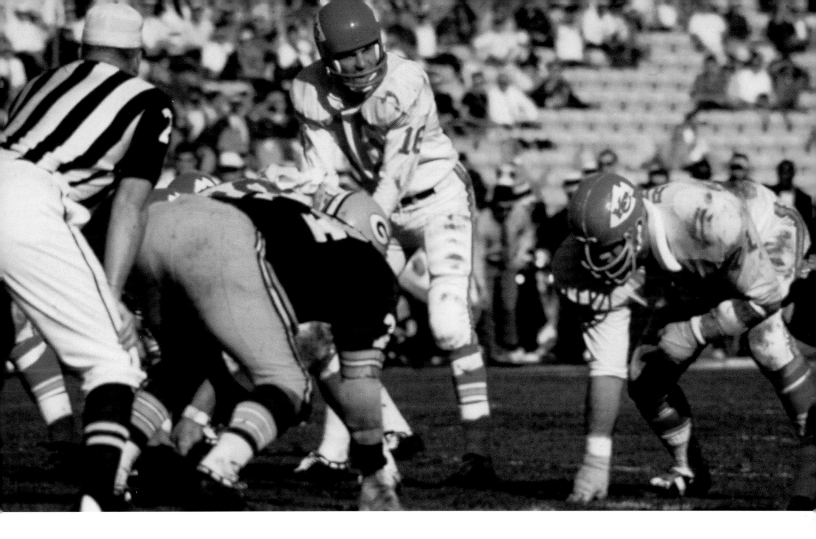

made fiscal sense. In 1966 Hunt, now the owner of the AFL's Kansas City Chiefs, and Tex Schramm, the general manager of the NFL's Dallas Cowboys, negotiated the details of the merger. On June 8, Rozelle, who had left the Rams in 1960 to become the NFL commissioner, announced that the two leagues would play a championship game at the end of the 1966 season, begin a unified draft in 1967 and officially merge into two conferences within a single league in 1970. Rozelle would stay on as commissioner of the new league.

The first AFL-NFL World Championship Game (it would be officially named the Super Bowl in 1969) was played on January 15, 1967, at Memorial Coliseum in Los Angeles, pitting the Green Bay Packers against the Kansas City Chiefs. NBC and CBS each paid the then-princely sum of $1 million to televise the game. The Packers came into the game as 14-point favorites, and despite a lackluster performance in the first half, they did not disappoint their fans. Little-used 34-year-old veteran wide receiver Max McGee was called into the game in the first quarter to replace the injured Boyd Dowler. McGee, who caught only four passes all season, never expected to play and had partied into the wee hours of the night before the game. Nursing a hangover, he not only played but played brilliantly, catching seven passes for 138 yards and two touchdowns. Among his catches was a sensational 37-yard touchdown grab in the first quarter. Quarterback Bart Starr threw behind McGee, and the hungover sub had to reach back across his body and make a one-handed catch. McGee described the play as follows: "It was a rotten pass, let's face it. You pay a guy $100,000 to throw to a $25,000 end, you expect him to put it right there. I was so sure the ball was going to be intercepted that I stuck out my hand and it stuck. Peo-

ple think it was planned; hell, that was an accident."

The Packers went on to steamroll the Chiefs in the second half and win Super Bowl I 35–10. Starr was as steady as ever, completing 16 of 23 passes for 250 yards while Green Bay's defense, led by snarling linebacker Ray Nitschke, held the Chiefs to just six first downs en route to shutting them out in the second half.

Green Bay returned to the Super Bowl the following season and won again in similar fashion, 33–14 over the Oakland Raiders. Several days later, Vince Lombardi, the Packers' legendary coach, announced his retirement from coaching to pursue front-office duties. With Lombardi gone and the Packers' nucleus aging fast, it was no longer a given that Green Bay would be the class of the NFL. It was, however, generally assumed that the NFL was still the AFL's superior. All such thoughts would soon change.

On January 12, 1969, the AFL's New York Jets faced off against the NFL's Baltimore Colts in Super Bowl III, and football fans everywhere settled in to watch the massacre. Baltimore, with its league-MVP quarterback, Earl Morrall, and its youthful yet disciplined coach, Don Shula, was considered by many to be one of the best football teams in history. Some oddsmakers had the Colts 18- to 20-point favorites prior to the game.

Predictions of a lopsided Colts win did little, however, to stop the brash 25-year-old Jets quarterback, Joe Namath, from publicly guaranteeing a New York victory. A balanced attack of Namath's passing (he completed 17 of 28 passes for 206 yards) and Matt Snell's rushing (30 carries for 121 yards and one score), coupled with an awful performance by Morrall, helped Namath and his team back up his guarantee with a stunning 16–7 upset.

The Jets win shattered all doubts about the legitimacy of the AFL. The party had grown a lot bigger, and the gate-crasher was now an honored guest.

Even NFL legend Johnny Unitas (No. 19, opposite) could not revive the Baltimore prospects in Super Bowl III; Namath's clutch performance on the field (above) led to his jubilant celebration off it (left) after New York's historic victory.

# Aftermath

Since the Packers in the 1960s, the Super Bowl has showcased several dominant teams, most notably the Pittsburgh Steelers, who won four times between 1975 and '80, the San Francisco 49ers, who won five titles between '82 and '95, and the Dallas Cowboys, who won three of four Super Bowls between '93 and '96. The Super Bowl is by far the most watched sporting event in the U.S., and the cost of a 30-second TV ad during its broadcast had risen to $1.6 million by 1999. Those who were outraged at the "exorbitant" $12 ticket price for Super Bowl I in 1967 would fall on their wallets at the sight of the $400 ticket for Super Bowl XXXIII in '99.

# THE BEATLES

"We don't think the Beatles will do anything in this market," Capitol Records president Alan Livingston told George Martin, the Beatles' producer, about the band's prospects in the United States. By November 1963, when Martin received that appraisal from Capitol, the Beatles had had three No. 1 hits in England and had inspired "Beatlemania," a term reporters coined after the crowds were turned away from the band's sold-out October 13 appearance on ITV's *Sunday Night at the London Palladium* and had become a mob of hysterical fans and bewildered police.

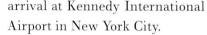

History may have backed up Livingston's assessment of the Beatles' chances in the States—where no British rock 'n' roll band had ever found success—but none of those other bands, of course, were the boyishly attractive and musically innovative Beatles. On January 25, 1964, "I Want to Hold Your Hand" hit the No. 1 spot on *Billboard*'s chart—a position the band would hold until May 9 with three different songs. Two weeks later 3,000 screaming Beatlemaniacs met John Lennon, Paul McCartney, George Harrison and Ringo Starr upon their arrival at Kennedy International Airport in New York City.

Such hysteria greeted the Beatles at every stop on their first tour of the States, which included three appearances on the *Ed Sullivan Show* and concerts in Washington, D.C., and New York City. Their buoyant, irreverent charm won over teens and the press alike. "Where did you get the idea for the haircuts?" asked one reporter at a press conference, referring to the Fab Four's famous shaggy "moptops." "Where did you get the idea for yours?" cheerfully retorted George. "Do you feel [your records] are musical?" asked another reporter; replied John, "Obviously they're musical. It's music, isn't it?"

**The Beatles (left, from top to bottom, John, Ringo, Paul and George) transformed rock 'n' roll in their Sgt. Pepper phase (above).**

*"The Beatles"*[TM] *Apple Corps Limited. "Yellow Submarine"*[TM] *Subafilms Limited.*

Beatlemania hit the United States with full force and included a concert in Shea Stadium (above), a splashy visit to Miami Beach (opposite), the appearance of Fab Four paraphernalia such as the Beatles button above and a rousing, scream-inducing televised visit to the *Ed Sullivan Show* (left).

# "We don't come to hear them, really. We have their records. We come to scream at them."

## —A BEATLES FAN, after a 1964 performance

As pop music, however, the Beatles' records were unusual. As Bob Dylan recalled, "They were doing things nobody was doing. Their chords were outrageous, just outrageous, and their harmonies made it all valid." And as Frank Zappa wrote in a 1968 article for *Life* magazine, "It was music made for young people by other young people.... It seemed to radiate a secret message: 'You can be free. You can get away with it. Look, we're doing it!' "

From the beginning, the Beatles were intent on performing their own material. Like many pop musicians at the time, from 1963 to '65 they released two new albums every year; unlike other pop musicians, however, they did not pad their albums with throwaway "filler" songs. Indeed, the first truly self-contained pop

music band, the Beatles were not only performers, but also brilliant songwriters. Released on December 6, 1965, *Rubber Soul* first revealed the startling widening of their artistic vision. They left behind the direct, feel-good songs like "I Want to Hold Your Hand" and began to write and record more ambiguous songs like "Norwegian Wood (This Bird Has Flown)," which, hinting at things to come, featured George on the sitar.

On August 29, 1966, the Beatles concluded their last tour in San Francisco's Candlestick Park. No longer committed to an exhausting performance schedule, they returned to Abbey Road Studios in late November and over the next five months recorded the album whose technical wizardry and conceptual unity transformed rock 'n'

roll, introducing to it a revolutionary array of musical structures and instruments. Framed as though it were a concert given by a fictional band, *Sgt. Pepper's Lonely Hearts Club Band* moves from song to song occasionally without "banding," or pauses, between them and features layers of sounds that could be produced only in a studio, such as the carnival of whirs and bells that jangle through "Being for the Benefit of Mr. Kite!" and the ascending orchestral cacophony that concludes "A Day in the Life." Even the album's lavish cover contributes to its concept: Costumed as Sgt. Pepper's band, the Beatles pose in front of an audience comprised of such figures as Sonny Liston, Edgar Allan Poe, and Marilyn Monroe.

Songs like "Within You Without You" reflected the surrealism and mysticism of the emerging counterculture, the exploration of

which brought the Beatles under the tutelage of Maharishi Mahesh Yogi; while on retreat with the guru in Wales, on August 27, 1967, they received the tragic news that their manager, Brian Epstein, had died.

Despite losing the manager who had guided them to their initial success, the Beatles continued to dominate and change the world of music with the groundbreaking albums *Yellow Submarine*, *The Beatles* (commonly known as "The White Album"), *Abbey Road*, and *Let it Be* and such massive-selling singles as "Hey Jude," "Something," and "Let it Be." In 1970, the band members separated and pursued solo careers, leaving behind them a legacy unsurpassed to this day of 14 U.S. No. 1 albums and 20 U.S. No. 1 singles—and justifiably earning the distinction as the most influential band in rock 'n' roll history.

# Aftermath

Brian Epstein (inset) helped engineer the Beatles' success, including their move into films such as *A Hard Day's Night* (opposite); the group's impromptu concert (above) on the roof of Apple's headquarters in London showcased material from their final album, aptly titled *Let it Be*.

From the '70s on, each of the Beatles enjoyed success as solo artists, rejecting pleas that they regroup—an act that became impossible after John Lennon was murdered in New York City on December 8, 1980. In 1995, however, Paul McCartney, George Harrison and Ringo Starr did come together to work as Beatles once more on two of John Lennon's unfinished songs, "Free as a Bird," and "Real Love"—which led the release of a three-album set, *The Beatles Anthology*. The three *Anthology* albums each went to No. 1 in the same year, a feat previously matched by only one band—the Beatles.

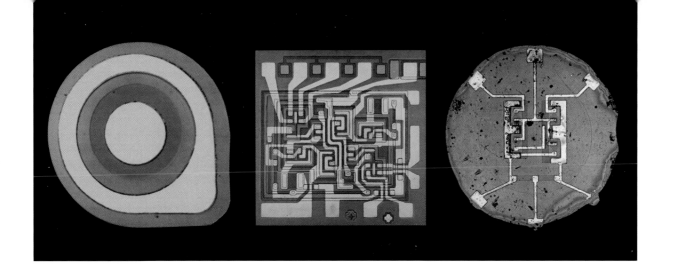

# THE INTEGRATED CIRCUIT

The success of the integrated circuit proves one thing definitively: Good things really do come in small packages. A small piece of silicon embedded with a complete electrical circuit, the integrated circuit, or IC, is the tiny hero of modern computing. Without it the electronics and computer industries of today would exist only in the minds of the most imaginative science fiction writers.

Invented in the 1940s, the first computers used vacuum tubes for processing electrical signals. The hulking machines weighed as much as 30 tons, filled entire rooms and had, by today's standards, a limited repertoire of mathematical functions. Costly to make and maintain, they also guzzled exorbitant amounts of energy and emitted vast quantities of heat.

The transistor, created at Bell Laboratories in December 1947, alleviated the energy consumption and emission problems. Far more compact and faster than vacuum tubes, the transistor was made from tiny pieces of semiconducting materials, such

as silicon or germanium, and gave off little heat. With the success of the transistor radio in the mid-'50s, the transistor became widespread, functioning as a key component in computers, televisions and virtually all electronic devices.

Unfortunately, the transistor was not foolproof. As engineers added more and more connections through soldering and wiring, the circuits became less and less reliable, a problem referred to in the electronics business as "the tyranny of numbers." The engineering community labored mightily to invent a structure that could contain and stabilize transistors and the myriad connections needed to operate new, sophisticated technologies.

The scientists at Fairchild Semiconductor went to work on the problem soon after the company was founded in Palo Alto, California, in 1957. Led by 29-year-old engineer Robert Noyce, the company made its first breakthrough with the development of flat transistors, which could be layered on top of one another, each transistor embedded in the one

**Noyce (left) and his early versions of the integrated circuit (above) revolutionized the computer industry.**

beneath. Fairchild soon applied this "planar" or "flat technique" to other components of the circuit. Next, Noyce hypothesized an entire circuit consisting of a single "block" of the semiconductor material—silicon—with no wires or soldering necessary.

One thousand miles away in Dallas, Jack Kilby, a young engineer at Texas Instruments, came up with precisely the same notion. He spent the summer concentrating on his idea, and his patent filing beat Noyce's by five months.

Both Fairchild and TI announced the invention of the integrated circuit in 1959. TI quickly filed a lawsuit against Fairchild for patent infringement, but the courts ruled in favor of Fairchild, acknowledging that each company had developed the new technology independently. In the future, any company with plans to use the integrated circuit in its products would have to obtain licenses from both Fairchild and TI.

Manufacturing the integrated circuit proved to be a delicate process. Even now, the IC must be made in a sterile environment because one speck of dust will contaminate its structure. The process begins with a thin piece of silicon that has been sliced from a long "log" of the material. One slice, or "wafer," yields several hundred chips. A maze of transistors, resistors and capacitators is then carefully etched into each section of the wafer.

Marketing the IC was a much easier task. Small, reliable and able to process data quickly without using much energy, it enabled computers to be incorporated into electrical devices like radios, jet aircraft and the Minuteman II missile. Not only did the IC make hand-held calculators and the first pacemaker possible, but the device also appeared in the first minicomputer in 1965 and powered the computer that guided NASA's Apollo 11 mission to the moon in July 1969.

Expensive at first, integrated circuits ranged in price from $120 to more than $1,000, depending on their complexity. Each contained an average of six active computer components per chip. That number doubled in subsequent years as engineers placed more circuits on thinner wafers of silicon. This innovation, coupled with increased demand, drove the IC's price down to less than $10 each by 1965.

Such developments fueled an entrepreneurial explosion in Palo Alto and its environs—christened

> **"If the auto industry had moved at the same speed... as our industry, your car today would cruise comfortably at a million miles an hour, [and] probably get half a million miles per gallon of gasoline."**
>
> *—GORDON MOORE, cofounder of Intel, on the semiconductor industry*

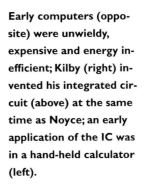

**Early computers (opposite) were unwieldy, expensive and energy inefficient; Kilby (right) invented his integrated circuit (above) at the same time as Noyce; an early application of the IC was in a hand-held calculator (left).**

Silicon Valley in the '70s—that continues today. During the mid- and late-'60s scores of Fairchild Semiconductor employees, nicknamed "Fairchildren," left the company to go into business for themselves. Two of them were Noyce and his colleague Gordon Moore. Together the pair formed their own semiconductor company, Intel (short for integrated electronics), in 1968. By the early 1970s Intel's integrated circuits became the standard for the industry.

Another revolution in the industry got under way when Intel engineer Ted Hoff proposed ICs equipped with circuitry that—unlike its predecessors, which were built to serve one particular purpose—could be programmed like a computer for any number of functions, whether they be calculating numbers or guiding a missile. Noyce, Intel's president, held to his conviction that the microprocessor would transform the computer and electronics industries, and by 1970 the company had produced a working model of what was referred to as "a computer on a chip." Little more than a decade later, the good thing in the small package allowed computers to be compact and affordable enough to be purchased for the home, sparking a personal computer boom.

# Aftermath

Integrated circuits and the device they spawned, the microprocessor, get smaller and faster every year. The integrated circuit of the '70s carried, on average, 50 elements. By the late '80s that number had increased to many hundreds of thousands. In 1997 the count was up to 7.5 million, and the Pentium III® processor released in 1999 boasted 9.5 million.

In addition to becoming speedier and more compact, computers have gotten smarter. In 1993 Intel unveiled the Pentium® processor, which allowed computers to process speech, sound, handwriting and photographs. The brains of the vast majority of personal computers, Intel's Pentium® series chips rule the semiconductor industry, and the company, with some $26 billion in net revenue in 1998, had more than 64,000 employees in 1999.

"Mother Fairchild" was taken over by one of its children, National Semiconductor, in 1987, only to be purchased by a venture capital group in 1998 and relaunched as an independent semiconductor manufacturer.

# THE VIETNAM WAR

The Vietnam War was the longest war the United States ever fought, and it was the first one the nation had lost in its 200-year history. Of the more than 3,000,000 American soldiers who served, 58,000 came home in body bags and aluminum coffins or were declared missing in action, and 300,000 more were wounded. The price of waging a losing war was estimated at a staggering $120 billion. But the terrible consequences of combat and the shortchanging of domestic needs were not the sum total of the evils the Vietnam War generated. It was the United States' most bitterly divisive conflict since the Civil War a hundred years earlier, inflicting political and social wounds that a quarter century later were still not completely healed.

Vietnam was part of the French colony of Indochina when, in 1950, the United States stepped into the quagmire. France's authority was under attack by local Communist insurgents led by Ho Chi Minh and backed by China and the U.S.S.R. Fearing that a Communist Vietnam would be a conduit for Red influence to other parts of Southeast Asia, President Harry Truman began sending military aid and advisers to bolster the French. These efforts were to no avail, however, for in 1954 Ho Chi Minh's insurgents routed the French. At the peace conference that oversaw the dismantling of French Indochina, Vietnam was divided into Communist North Vietnam and American-supported South Vietnam.

But the Communists of South Vietnam, called the Vietcong or the National Liberation Front, were fiercely nationalistic, and they were determined to overthrow the South's government, expel the Americans and reunite their divided country. Fighting between the South's army and the Vietcong mounted steadily. The South Vietnamese troops, ill motivated and poorly led,

As the number of American troops and helicopters escalated (top), so did the terrible toll taken on the soldiers (left).

deserted in droves. By the end of 1963, the number of American advisers in South Vietnam stood at 17,000, with $500 million in aid having been poured into the country in that year alone, but much of the countryside was now under Communist control.

Behind closed doors, President Lyndon Johnson said that he didn't think Vietnam—a "little piss-ant country," in his opinion—was worth fighting for. But conservatives were pressuring him to "Americanize" the war, and he knew that resistance to such a policy might provoke political and military leaders favoring escalation to sabotage his ambitious social programs. Moreover, the presidential campaign was fast approaching, and with it the specter of Republicans labeling him "soft on communism" if he sought to disentangle the U.S. from its commitments in Vietnam.

Within a year, Johnson vastly increased the American presence in Vietnam. Although Congress never officially declared war, it did pass the Gulf of Tonkin Resolution, which gave the president authority to "take all necessary measures to repel any armed attack against the forces of the United States and to prevent further aggression." In March 1965 Johnson sent the first U.S. ground troops, 3,500 marines, to Vietnam, and by year's end the number of military personnel had swelled to 184,000.

At the same time, North Vietnam was sending thousands of troops south along the Ho Chi Minh Trail to fight alongside the Vietcong. Fighting almost never took place along a battle line. Instead it often began when the enemy emerged from the jungle and ambushed an American patrol. Helicopters would ferry in reinforcements,

> "I am not going to lose Vietnam. I am not going to be the President who saw Southeast Asia go the way China went."
>
> —*PRESIDENT LYNDON JOHNSON, 1963*

Whether wading through waist-high rushes (left, in An-Khe), being dropped into combat by a helicopter (opposite, in the Ashau Valley) or simply trying to survive amidst the wreckage and the war-ravaged landscape (above, in Quang Tri), American troops were faced with nightmarish battlefield conditions.

but after an exchange of fire, the Communist soldiers would slip back into the jungle, ending the skirmish. Because fighting did not take place along a conventional front, the results could not be measured in territory gained or lost. Instead, the military assessed combat in terms of "body count" and "kill ratio," which measured the number of enemy dead for each American lost.

And it was all too often impossible to be sure exactly who the enemy was. The Vietcong did not wear uniforms, making it difficult to distinguish them from ordinary citizens. One marine captain recalled, "You never knew who was the enemy and who was the friend. They all dressed alike."

The U.S. mounted a bombing campaign of extraordinary ferocity. Between 1965 and the end of 1967 alone, more American bombs were dropped on Vietnam than had been used in all of

World War II. Millions upon millions of acres of forest were destroyed, and a quarter of the South's population was uprooted. But the war dragged on, with no signs of flagging enemy resolve. In increasing numbers Americans, the majority of whom had supported sending combat troops to Vietnam in 1965, began to question why the nation should continue what seemed an open-ended conflict.

But American politicians and military leaders lagged far behind the public's growing antiwar sentiment. Elected president in 1968, Richard Nixon began bringing troops home under his policy of "Vietnamization." But the last of them did not ship out until 1973, when the U.S. and the North Vietnamese finally negotiated a cease-fire. The future of South Vietnam rested in the hands of its leaders.

The fighting created millions of refugees, including a family fleeing American bombs outside Qui Nhon (opposite) and the hundreds of displaced people departing Saigon (left) in the wake of Vietcong attacks in 1968; in the end the poorly motivated South Vietnamese troops (bottom) could not prevent the fall of the South and the departure of the Americans, many of whom left from the roof of the U.S. embassy (below).

# Aftermath

Following the withdrawal of American forces, the war continued until 1975, when the North Vietnamese overwhelmed the troops defending Saigon, the capital of South Vietnam, and overran the city. On May 1, the triumphant northerners raised their flag in Saigon, which they renamed Ho Chi Minh City in honor of their leader. After two decades of carnage in which some 4,000,000 Vietnamese—northerners, southerners, civilians and soldiers—lost their lives, the two Vietnams became a single nation, under Communist rule.

# BARBIE® DOLL

Slumber parties across America moved a notch higher on the good-time scale once Barbie Millicent Roberts® hit the social circuit in the early 1960s. Lounging in her tricot baby doll nightie and matching bloomers, golden hair swept back from her creamy face, she seemed to listen to and even inspire the twittering girl talk. Without Barbie®, the Wisconsin girl from Willows High, the party would surely be a flop.

Before Barbie® doll's debut, baby dolls and paper dolls reigned atop the mountain of girls' toys. And while Barbie® doll's entrance didn't unseat Betsy Wetsy and Jo the paper doll, it did shift the industry's emphasis from a girl's maternal instincts to her more material concerns, like careful grooming—evidenced in Barbie® doll's miniature combs, brushes and handkerchiefs—and ladylike poise.

Not the sort of role model one would expect to emerge from a small apartment in a former Chinese laundry in Los Angeles. But it was there that husband-and-wife team Elliot and Ruth Handler began making and selling gift items in the late 1930s. Their humble cottage industry blossomed into the Mattel toy company in 1945, with Elliot in charge of design and Ruth in charge of sales. Ruth was convinced that little girls needed a more adult doll to play with, particularly after watching her daughter and her playmates acting the roles of college students and career women using the only teenage and adult figures at hand—limited, one-dimensional paper dolls. This pretend play started Ruth thinking about a grown-up doll, small enough to fit into a child's hand yet large enough to dress with ease.

She happened upon an incarnation of her idea in a Swiss toy store while vacationing in Europe in 1956. The Bild Lilli, as it was called, was the three-dimensional spinoff of a German comic strip char-

**Barbie® (left, with Ken®, and above, from left to right in 1959, '66 and '68) fueled the fantasies of generations of girls.**

"We introduced Barbie® with a big splash. And to our surprise, 25 percent of the retailers refused to carry her and another 25 percent were reluctant. They said she wouldn't sell because she had breasts."

—*RUTH HANDLER, cofounder of Mattel Toys, in* Adweek, *November 1987*

acter named Lilli. When she spied her 13-year-old daughter, Barbara, vacillating among the beautifully buxom 11½-inch Lilli dolls in an attempt to choose her favorite outfit, Ruth quickly decided her doll would have a wardrobe that could be purchased separately from the doll.

Ruth's efforts to enter the doll market were initially opposed by the company's designers, who were more accustomed to creating jack-in-the-boxes and cap pistols and who worried that high production costs on the Barbie® doll would yield an expensive doll. But Handler pressed on regardless

and finally persuaded Mattel's all-male design team at the company's headquarters in Hawthorne, a Los Angeles suburb, to produce the Barbie® doll.

Two years later, in March 1959, the all-American girl emerged from the Kokusai Boeki Kaisha Ltd. plant in Japan and jetted to New York City for her first public appearance at the American International Toy Fair. The doll, named after the Handlers' daughter, made a striking debut with her narrow waist, long tapered legs and high-heeled shoes. Detailed facial features and painted finger- and toenails accented Barbie® doll's image.

Accompanied by 22 outfits, Barbie® doll met with mixed reviews. Retail buyers were skeptical that the small, 11½-inch doll with an ample bosom—the Barbie® doll was the first American children's doll to have breasts—would charm the target audience, girls aged three to 11. As a result, only half of the buyers placed orders for the $3 doll.

But girls quickly proved the skeptics wrong. By Christmas Barbie® doll was the hottest toy on the market, and at year's end Mattel had sold 351,000 Barbie® dolls, a number that grew to five million only four years later.

Every girl needs a guy, of course, and Barbie® doll's was Ken® doll, named after the Handler's son Kenneth. The first Ken® doll, introduced in 1961, had fuzzy hair and a slight frame. His pale, expressionless face didn't faze Barbie® doll or her fans, who eagerly snatched Ken® doll off toy-store shelves during his first year on the market.

A boyfriend was not the only companion Mattel envisioned for Barbie® doll. Released in 1963, two years after the Barbie® Dream House®, was Midge® doll, Barbie® doll's freckle-faced best friend and first houseguest. To girls' delight, Midge® doll's clothes were the same size as Barbie® doll's, so they could swap outfits. Skipper® doll, Barbie® doll's little sister, joined the group in 1964.

In step with the social currents of the decade, Mattel made changes to the Barbie® doll throughout the '60s. Bendable legs, a twisting waist and a new, younger-looking face rounded out the doll's physical and cosmetic alterations. The improvements prompted Mattel to allow girls to trade in their "old" Barbie® dolls and buy the new one for $1.50. More than one million dolls were handed over in May 1967 alone.

Despite Barbie® doll's popularity, critics contended that her voluptuous figure damaged girls' self-esteem by representing unattainable proportions. Outfits depicting Barbie® in such

**Barbie® (left) and her wardrobe (inset) debuted in 1959; new versions appeared in 1962 (below), '67 (opposite, left), and '69 (opposite, right) and a friend, Casey® doll (opposite, inset), appeared in '67; the idea for Barbie® doll came from Ruth Handler (opposite, top, with husband and Mattel cofounder Elliot).**

roles as "Career Girl" and veterinarian did little to alter her image as a curvaceous gal-pal.

But the girls who spent hours and hours in fantasy play with their Barbie® dolls beg to differ. Even though their fantasies about adult life changed as they matured, they remember their hours with Barbie® doll as vital to the development of their imaginations—not to mention to the success of those otherwise lackluster slumber parties.

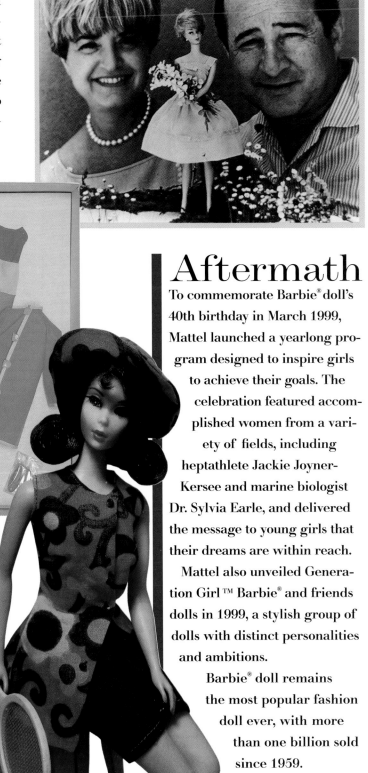

# Aftermath

To commemorate Barbie® doll's 40th birthday in March 1999, Mattel launched a yearlong program designed to inspire girls to achieve their goals. The celebration featured accomplished women from a variety of fields, including heptathlete Jackie Joyner-Kersee and marine biologist Dr. Sylvia Earle, and delivered the message to young girls that their dreams are within reach.

Mattel also unveiled Generation Girl™ Barbie® and friends dolls in 1999, a stylish group of dolls with distinct personalities and ambitions.

Barbie® doll remains the most popular fashion doll ever, with more than one billion sold since 1959.

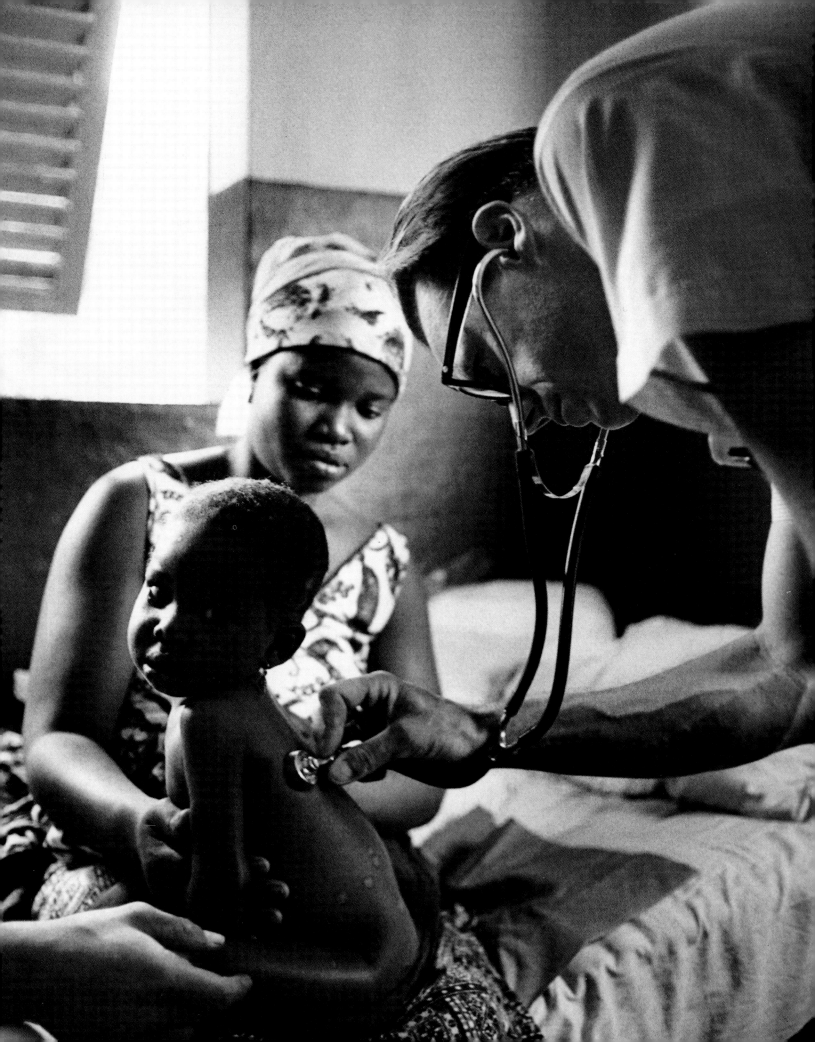

# THE PEACE CORPS

Everyone needs a purpose in life, something of value that sustains the individual beyond the basic physical needs of the body. President John F. Kennedy counted on that when he appealed to the men and women of America to help others in foreign lands as volunteers in his brainchild, the Peace Corps.

Kennedy first raised the idea of the Peace Corps during an impromptu speech in the early morning hours of October 14, 1960, when he challenged a group of students at the University of Michigan to give 10 years of their lives to help people in developing countries. Thousands of letters of interest awaited him when he arrived at the White House three months later as the newly elected president.

Kennedy tapped his 44-year-old brother-in-law, businessman Sargent Shriver, to structure the proposed organization. At Shriver's urging, the president signed Executive Order 10924 on March 1, 1961, creating the Peace Corps on a temporary pilot basis pending a congressional vote. The Senate officially proposed the program on August 25, and the House voted it into law on September 14, 1961.

The Peace Corps began with three goals: to promote world peace and friendship by making Americans available to help other countries meet their needs for trained manpower; to promote a better understanding of the American people among the people served; and to promote a better understanding of foreign lands and peoples within the American public.

Radio and television stations broadcast public service announcements, and 80,000 signs were posted on municipal transit routes and college campuses to attract the volunteers needed to meet Shriver's goal of having 650 volunteers in the field by January 1962. More than 32,000 people applied for a 27-month tour—three months of training, 24 months in the field—and by July '61, 52 trainees were at

**The ranks of volunteers grew after Kennedy bid the first group farewell (above), eventually including doctors in Togo (left).**

*The Peace Corps in Ethiopia © 1966 The Norman Rockwell Family Trust.*

the University of California at Berkeley preparing for their assignments in the West African nation of Ghana. Volunteers, all U.S. citizens at least 18 years old, underwent rigorous physical training and instruction in the local language and in the jobs they would be perfoming in the host country. Ghana expressed a need for electricians, teachers and plumbers. With his available recruits, Shriver could only accommodate the request for teachers. The lack of skilled manual laborers would continue to plague the Peace Corps throughout its existence.

Members of the first class of Peace Corps volunteers—or Ghana I, as they were nicknamed—each shook hands with President Kennedy at the White House before boarding a jet for Africa. Once in their host country, volunteers were expected to create their own jobs. This was one of the greater challenges for Peace Corps volunteers, especially those assigned to "community development," a somewhat loosely defined role that called for individuals to organize community activities that would motivate the local participants to take greater control of their lives.

As the number of Peace Corps volunteers swelled, the program came under increasing criticism for being unnecessarily large and too informal. Though some early host nations such as Malaysia and Ghana had clearly defined pro-

"To those peoples
in the huts and
villages of half the
globe struggling to
break the bonds of
mass misery, we
pledge our best
efforts to help them
help themselves...."
—*JOHN F. KENNEDY,*
*January 20, 1961*

**Early Peace Corps volunteers included teachers in Peru (opposite), Bolivia (above, teaching modern methods of sheep shearing) and Nepal (right, at the nation's only teacher training college, and top right, teaching biology).**

grams, others were in disarray. In Pakistan, for example, Peace Corps evaluation staff reported that only 16 of 61 volunteers had serious jobs.

Despite the criticism, eager volunteers put the organization's slogan "the toughest job you'll ever love" to the test. They built the first A-frame dwelling in Sierra Leone, helped villagers raise chickens and trawl for fish in Togo, cared for infants in Malaysian leprosariums, instructed

The mission of *los hijos de Kennedy*, or "children of Kennedy," as volunteers were called in Latin America, received a grievous blow when the man who had inspired them to volunteer was assassinated on November 22, 1963. But his death only served to amplify his call to service. In the seven days that followed Kennedy's assassination, the Peace Corps received 2,550 applications, the most ever logged in one week. The following year, applications reached an all-time high of 45,653.

In spite of the growing unrest that was sweeping the nation, the Peace Corps continued its work during Lyndon Johnson's presidency, and in 1966 the number of volunteers in the field reached 15,556, a record number that still stands.

Dominican women on how to market clay pots and taught school in every host country. Volunteers often had to adjust to a slower pace of life where the day began at 5 A.M., the floors were made of dirt and the only entertainment was a village wedding. Primitive conditions and disorganization aside, most former volunteers describe their experience as a great adventure that changed their lives.

As the younger generation grew more radical, so too did the tenor of the Peace Corps volunteers, with earnest idealists giving way to antiwar radicals as the decade progressed. But even a foe as powerful as President Johnson's successor, Richard Nixon, could not stifle the organization. For a purpose still existed, and the committed volunteers, the true architects of the Peace Corps, knew what they had to do.

Volunteer John Soldate taught math in Botswana (opposite, top), Dennis Shaner was a mechanic at an agricultural training farm in Tunisia (opposite, bottom) and Willie Douglas (at right in photo at left) taught agricultural science in Pakistan.

# Aftermath

Since the inception of the Peace Corps, volunteers have served in 134 countries. Although the number of applications never again reached the level of the early 1960s, the number of volunteers in the field has hovered between 5,000 and 7,000 since the early '70s. As of 1999, the Peace Corps had 7,400 volunteers stationed in 80 countries.

Projects of the late '80s and '90s included environmental work, but teachers remain a mainstay of the Peace Corps, with approximately 40 percent of volunteers in 1998 working in education.

Former volunteers who continued to serve their country include Donna Shalala (Iran, 1962-64), Secretary of Health and Human Services in the Clinton Administration, and senators Christopher Dodd (Dominican Republic, 1966-68) and the late Paul Tsongas (Ethiopia, 1962-64).

# ROGER MARIS, 61 IN '61

Mark McGwire and Sammy Sosa breathed new life into the game of baseball during the summer of 1998. Their spectacular pursuit of Roger Maris's single-season home run record helped fans forget the bitter players' strike of 1994.

While McGwire and Sosa were treated like conquering heroes in ballparks across the nation, Maris, during his pursuit in 1961, was treated like a thief in the temple. Where Mac and Sammy were showered with adulation, Maris got aggravation—and sometimes defamation. He was challenging the milestone of 60  homers in a season established in 1927 by the legendary Babe Ruth, and no one, it seemed, wanted him to succeed.

Even in his home stadium—it wasn't called the House That Ruth Built for nothing—Maris was treated like an interloper. Yankee fans evidently felt that if the Bambino's record had to fall, it should go to Maris's teammate Mickey Mantle, a lifetime Yankee and the heir to Joe DiMaggio, who was also on pace for the record that year. Who was this newcomer Maris, a mere .260 hitter, to challenge the Babe? "I was booed for 81 games at home and 81 games on the road," Maris said. "You say it doesn't affect you, but it does."

A reticent, plain-spoken man who grew up in Fargo, North Dakota, Maris had been traded to the Yankees from the Kansas City Athletics in 1960. Craftsmanlike, unflashy, he excelled in the finer points of the game, skills such as baserunning, fielding and throwing, that don't always show up in the box score. But he was also a feared batter. His routine before stepping into the batter's box spoke volumes about his game, not to mention his personality: one or two warmup swings and Maris was ready to hit. There were no elaborate waggles, no arabesques traced in the air with his bat. He was the same way with the press, to whom he spoke with an arresting candor that rubbed some scribes

**Maris (opposite, right) and Mantle (opposite, left) kept the Yankee dugout (above) applauding all season long.**

*©1999 Roger Maris Family. Made under license with Mrs. Roger Maris. Major League Baseball trademarks and copyrights are used with permission of Major League Baseball Properties, Inc.*

the wrong way. Perhaps this was why some wags, and many fans, deemed Maris unworthy of Ruth's legacy. It couldn't have been his performance: In his first year in pinstripes, Maris drove in 112 runs, belted 39 homers and was named MVP of the American League.

As his homer total mounted in '61, the lack of appreciation turned into outright disrespect. One reporter asked Maris, "How come a .260 hitter like you manages to get more home runs than Babe Ruth?" Incredulous, Maris had to put up with this line of inquiry all summer. The age of the press conference had yet to dawn, so reporters simply massed at Maris's locker, coming at him in waves. Those at the back couldn't hear what was being said up front, and when their turn came, they

invariably repeated questions Maris had answered several times already. "He was half goofy by the end of the season," said Maris's father, Rudy.

Still, he hit home runs with clockwork regularity, and the Yankees marched toward the pennant. Maris and Mantle became known as the M&M Boys. During one midseason stretch, Maris parked 24 home runs in 38 games.

As if the fans and the media rooting against him weren't enough, Maris had another opponent in baseball commissioner Ford Frick. Since the schedule had been expanded from 154 games to 162 that year, Frick, an old crony of Ruth's, ruled that if the record was broken after the 154th game of the season, two milestones would be listed—one for a 154-game season, and one for a 162-game season.

Maris's powerful swing (opposite) helped him surpass Babe Ruth (left, on plaque in Yankee Stadium) and made Maris the new single-season home run king (above); the price of Maris's run at the record was exhaustion (below).

"A lot of people in this country must think it's a crime to have anyone break Ruth's record."

—*ROGER MARIS, prior to the 154th game of the 1961 season when he, two homers short of the record, received two dozen letters and six telegrams wishing him ill.*

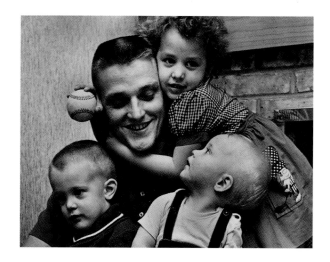

As formidable a slugger as Maris (above) was, for most of his career he was better known as an all-around player, who rarely made mistakes and occasionally contributed a great defensive play such as the catch at right; Maris's mainstay throughout his ordeal was his wife, Pat (opposite, right).

As the pressure built, Maris started losing his hair in clumps. He entered September with 51 homers, eight ahead of Ruth's pace. Mantle got injured and dropped out of the race with 54 homers. Maris forged ahead alone. The 154th game of the year came on September 20 in Baltimore, Ruth's birthplace. Maris's total stood at 58. He hit his 59th homer in the third inning and made a warning-track out in the seventh. The Yanks won 4–2 and clinched the pennant. Headlines the following day declared MARIS FAILS.

He belted No. 60 on September 26, and on October 1, in the last game of the regular season, Maris sent a 2–0 fastball from Boston righthander Tracy Stallard into the rightfield stands at Yankee Stadium for No. 61. Incredibly, only 23,154 fans, slightly less than a third of capacity, attended the game. Undersized but appreciative, they gave Maris a standing ovation. He said that he "went blank" as he rounded the bases. His teammates had to push him out of the dugout so he could bask in the cheers.

Most observers, citing the expanded schedule, assumed the record wouldn't last, certainly not as long as the 34 years Ruth's had. Devalued by Frick's asterisk until 1991, Maris's record lasted 37 years.

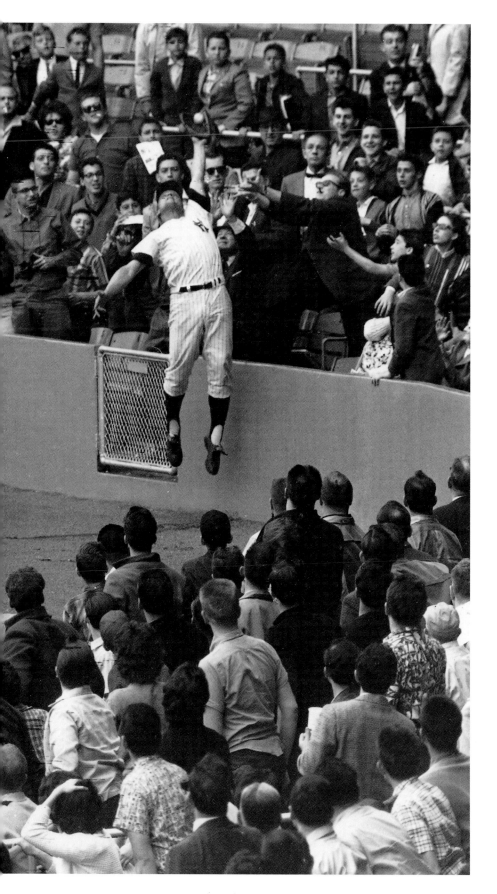

# Aftermath

The Yankees went on to win the 1961 World Series in five games over the Cincinnati Reds, as Maris belted a game-winning homer in Game 3. In 1962, Maris helped the Yankees to another title, hitting 33 homers and driving in 100 runs. Despite his worthy qualifications—back-to-back MVP awards, seven World Series appearances in 12 years, the home run record—Maris has not been elected to the Baseball Hall of Fame.

In 1984, Yankees owner George Steinbrenner erected a plaque to Maris in Yankee Stadium, alongside tributes to Ruth, Mantle and DiMaggio. It reads in part, "In belated recognition of one of baseball's greatest achievements."

Maris died of cancer in 1985 at the age of 51. His six children watched from the front row in St. Louis's Busch Stadium as McGwire broke their father's record on September 8, 1998. McGwire invited them onto the field to join the postgame ceremony marking the occasion.

# WOODSTOCK

Cram half a million people into an area meant for one-third that number, add heavy traffic, torrential rain and sloppy mud, then deprive the participants of food, fresh water and shelter. Under most circumstances that combination is a recipe for disaster, if not a full-scale riot. But from August 15 to 17, 1969, in upstate New York, those conditions, coupled with some superb music, made for the greatest single concert event of all time.

The concept for the Woodstock Music and Art Fair was the brainchild of four men: Michael Lang, a sometime band manager and ex-head shop proprietor; Artie Kornfeld, a former executive with Capitol Records; and business partners Joel Rosenman and John Roberts, founders of JR Capital Corp. and Mediasound Recording Studios. They set their sights on Woodstock, New York, as the venue. Together the foursome planned a three-day outdoor concert reminiscent of California's Monterey Pop Festival

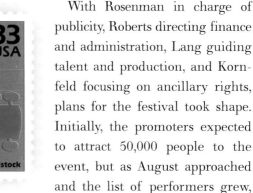

of 1967. When they couldn't find an appropriate venue in Woodstock, the promoters moved the event 45 miles southwest to the town of Bethel, where local farmer Max Yasgur leased his land for the sum of $50,000.

With Rosenman in charge of publicity, Roberts directing finance and administration, Lang guiding talent and production, and Kornfeld focusing on ancillary rights, plans for the festival took shape. Initially, the promoters expected to attract 50,000 people to the event, but as August approached and the list of performers grew, so did their estimate of attendance. A week prior to August 15, they were prepared to accommodate up to 150,000 people. By Wednesday the 13th, there were already roughly 60,000 people assembled at Yasgur's farm without a single ticket having been collected. On Friday, as people kept coming and attendance showed signs of swelling to its eventual total of almost 500,000 people, the pro-

**The gigantic crowds (opposite and above) that flocked to Woodstock enjoyed one of rock's most unforgettable concerts.**

*Woodstock and the guitar-and-dove logo are registered trademarks of Woodstock Ventures LC.*

moters abandoned the notion of collecting the $18 tickets and announced what everyone already knew: Woodstock would be a free concert.

The music was scheduled to start at 4 P.M. on Friday, but the throng of revelers headed to Woodstock brought most ground transportation into Bethel to a stop. Thousands of people left their cars along Route 17B and walked the rest of the way to Bethel. Due to the traffic, most of the musicians, including early arrival Richie Havens, had to be flown by helicopter to the site. As soon as Lang saw Havens, he pleaded with him to go onstage and start the concert, which was now an hour behind schedule. Havens, originally slated to go on fifth, agreed to open but told Lang, "The first beer can that comes up onstage, Michael, you're gonna owe me, 'cuz your concert is late, and they're gonna get me for it." The beer cans never flew, and Havens kicked off three days of peace and music.

Woodstock featured a diverse and impressive array of performers. After Havens on Day One came such artists as Country Joe McDonald, who performed his popular antiwar song, "I-Feel-Like-I'm-Fixin'-to-Die Rag," Ravi Shankar, whose sitar set

| Woodstock Music and Art Fair | Woodstock Music and Art Fair | Woodstock Music and Art Fair | THREE DAY TICKET |
|---|---|---|---|
| **FRIDAY** | **SATURDAY** | **SUNDAY** | |
| August 15, 1969 10 A. M. | August 16, 1969 10 A. M. | August 17, 1969 10 A. M. | Aug. 15, 16, 17 1969 |
| **$6.00** | **$6.00** | **$6.00** | **$18.00** |
| Good For One Admission Only | Good For One Admission Only | Good For One Admission Only | |
| 15296 NO REFUNDS | 15296 NO REFUNDS | 15296 NO REFUNDS | 15296 |

The promotional posters (below, left) helped attract far larger crowds to Woodstock than anticipated, creating horrendous traffic jams (left) and making ticket sales (above) practically impossible; in spite of it all, fans (below and opposite, far left) had an unforgettable experience.

WOODSTOCK MUSIC & ART FAIR
presents

**AN AQUARIAN EXPOSITION**
in
**WHITE LAKE, N.Y.**

**3DAYS
of PEACE
&MUSIC**

**WITH**

| | | |
|---|---|---|
| Joan Baez | Keef Hartley | The Band |
| Arlo Guthrie | Canned Heat | Jeff Beck Group |
| Tim Hardin | Creedence Clearwater | Blood, Sweat and Tears |
| Richie Havens | Grateful Dead | Joe Cocker |
| Incredible String Band | Janis Joplin | Crosby, Stills and Nash |
| Ravi Shankar | Jefferson Airplane | Jimi Hendrix |
| Sly And The Family Stone | Mountain | Iron Butterfly |
| Bert Sommer | Quill | Ten Years After |
| Sweetwater | Santana | Johnny Winter |
| | The Who | |

**FRI.
AUG. 15** | **SAT.
AUG. 16** | **SUN.
AUG. 17**

All programs subject to change without notice
*White Lake, Town of Bethel, Sullivan County, N.Y.

"Like I was rapping to the fuzz. Can you dig it? Man, there's supposed to be a million and a half people here by tonight. Can you dig that? The New York State Thruway is closed, man."

—*ARLO GUTHRIE, August 15, 1969*

65

was rained on—this would be a recurring theme at Woodstock—and folk star Arlo Guthrie, who famously announced to the crowd that the New York State Thruway was closed. Day Two featured several electrifying performances, including Santana's percussion-heavy "Soul Sacrifice" and Sly and the Family Stone's infectious "I Want to Take You Higher," not to mention The Who's Pete Townshend and his signature guitar-bashing act.

The immense crowd of spectators, packed as tight as could be and stretching over the horizon, enjoyed the music and each other. Despite the shortages of food, shelter and water, they managed to have the time of their lives. Hearing of the need for food, residents from the surrounding area made sandwiches and hard-boiled eggs; the U.S. Army and National Guard also flew in additional food and medical supplies. It was one big survival party. While the music played, people smoked, drank, took psychedelic drugs and had sex.

On Sunday, Joe Cocker sang a rousing cover of the Beatles' "A Little Help From My Friends," which perfectly reflected the cooperative good feeling of the weekend. Following Cocker, the skies opened up and heavy rains pelted the proceedings. Scores of people took to the muddy conditions like giddy pigs, singing and splashing around in the slop of Yasgur's farm. After another long day and night of music, most of those in attendance began to pack up and leave Bethel. The 30,000 or so who stuck around awoke on Monday morning to hear Jimi Hendrix close the concert with a set that included an incendiary electric-guitar version of "The Star Spangled Banner."

The following year Hendrix and fellow Woodstock performers Janis Joplin and Al Wilson of Canned Heat would all suffer drug-related deaths, a sobering wake-up call for the psychedelic '60s dream. While Woodstock may not have changed the world, it did provide a face and a voice for a misunderstood generation and gave the country a glimpse of peace and harmony at the end of a tumultuous decade.

# Aftermath

Staging a free concert left Woodstock promoters Roberts and Rosenman very much in the red. Suppliers were clamoring to be paid, and Yasgur's farm was in need of a major cleanup. Convinced that declaring bankruptcy would be ducking their responsibilities not only to their creditors but to the integrity of the event, they sold nearly all of their interest in the film and record of the event to Warner Bros. for $1 million. That money, together with additional funds borrowed from Roberts's family, was used to pay every outstanding bill and to restore the farmland that had been the festival's home that historic summer.

**Among the stunning array of performers at Woodstock were Havens (opposite, above), who opened the show, and** **Hendrix (top), who closed it with a now-classic electric version of "The Star Spangled Banner"; also appearing were Joplin** **(opposite, below), Jerry Garcia (above, left), Guthrie (above, middle), Joan Baez (above, right) and Cocker (right).**

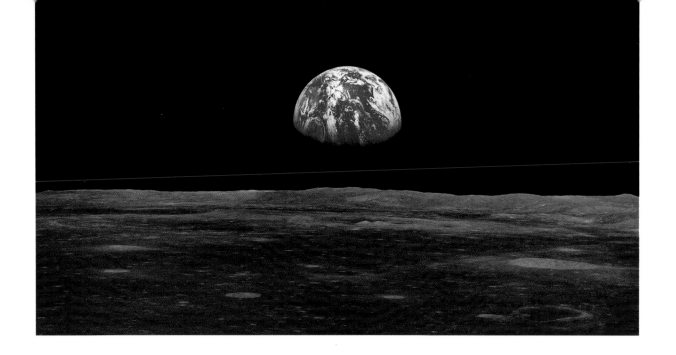

# MAN WALKS ON THE MOON

Prodded by President John F. Kennedy to challenge the Soviet Union's supremacy in space, the United States jumped into a race against the Soviets in 1961 to put a man on the Moon by the end of the decade. When Apollo 11 astronauts Michael Collins, Neil Armstrong and Edwin "Buzz" Aldrin blasted off from the Kennedy Space Center in Florida aboard the spacecraft *Columbia* on July 16, 1969, their goal was to meet the president's challenge, in NASA's terse phrase, to "perform a manned lunar landing and return."

Two months earlier, the crew of Apollo 10 had run through a dress rehearsal that stopped, as planned, just short of an actual landing, with two astronauts taking their landing craft down to within nine miles of the Moon's surface before returning to the mother ship.

Now it was up to the Apollo 11 crew to go that final distance—a feat that would be the greatest of great adventures. But Collins, the Apollo 11 command module pilot, was wary of predicting so triumphant an outcome. Well aware of how many things could go wrong, he privately concluded that he "wouldn't give better than even odds on a successful landing and return."

The first three days of the 240,000-mile flight were free of serious hitches, and by the fourth the Moon had grown from a little yellow disk to a gigantic, bulging globe. Jagged rock formations, huge craters and razor-sharp shadows filled the window the three awe-struck astronauts peered through, and it came home forcefully to Collins that he and his fellow crew members were "about to lay our little pink bodies on the line" in an alien environment filled with incalculable risks.

**Aldrin (opposite) stood on the Moon, whose shadow partially covered the Earth in the Apollo 11 photo above.**

# "Apollo represents a positively mythic accomplishment for the human species. The Moon was the metaphor of the unattainable." —*CARL SAGAN, astronomer*

After easing *Columbia* into orbit around the Moon, the astronauts checked out the lunar lander, *Eagle*. All systems were go. The astronauts spent the night in orbit aboard *Columbia*, 60 miles above the Moon, and the next day, July 20, Armstrong and Aldrin squeezed into *Eagle* through its tiny hatch. Now alone in *Columbia*, Collins threw a switch, and as the lunar lander began moving away from *Columbia*, an exultant Armstrong cried, "The *Eagle* has wings!"

An automatic navigation system guided the lander toward a site on the Sea of Tranquillity that had been chosen because it appeared to be fairly level and free of rubble. As they neared the landing site, however, Armstrong and Aldrin realized that they were headed for a treacherous-looking crater as big as a football field. Overriding the automatic system, Armstrong grabbed the

On July 16, 1969, staff members at the Kennedy Space Center stood from their computer consoles to watch the Apollo 11 liftoff through windows looking out onto the launch pad (opposite); four days later, wearing a backpack filled with life-support equipment, Aldrin backed down the lunar lander's ladder (left) to join Neil Armstrong, who snapped the photo of his fellow crew member; below, an astronaut's footprint was stamped in moon dust.

After the *Columbia*'s mid-Pacific splashdown, the astronauts waited in a raft (left) with a navy swimmer for a helicopter to fly them to the U.S.S. *Hornet;* quarantined on the *Hornet* in case they were carrying alien bacteria, Armstrong, Collins and Aldrin (below, left to right) communicated from behind a window; three weeks later, New York City honored the trio with a ticker-tape parade (opposite).

controls and flew *Eagle* past the crater to a site that looked smoother. As they neared the surface of the Sea of Tranquillity, the engine exhaust whipped up a cloud of moon dust.

At NASA's Mission Control in Houston, the staff listened tensely to Aldrin narrating *Eagle*'s descent: "Seventy-five feet ... lights on ... down two and a half ... 40 feet? ... kicking up some dust ... 30 feet ... drifting to the right a little ... contact light ... okay. Engine stop." After a brief pause, Armstrong said, "Houston, Tranquillity Base here. The *Eagle* has landed!"

Armstrong clambered down *Eagle*'s ladder first. He switched on a television camera attached to the lander, and when both of his feet were planted on the Moon's powdery surface, he declared, "That's one small step for man, one giant leap for mankind." Back on Earth, a half-billion people watched the extraordinary moment on television.

Buoyant, goose-pimply with excitement and marveling at the "magnificent desolation" extending in every direction, Aldrin joined Armstrong on the lunar surface. Getting down to work, they erected an American flag equipped with a horizontal telescoping arm to make it appear to be waving in the near-vacuum of the Moon's atmosphere. They couldn't push the flagpole far enough into the surface to keep it steady, and Aldrin was in dread that it would fall over while the television camera was trained on it. (It stayed upright during the broadcast, only to col-

lapse later when blasted by the thrust of *Eagle*'s engine when the crew lifted off.)

During their two and a half hours of moon-walking, Armstrong and Aldrin set up a reflector that would bounce laser beams back to Earth and allow scientists to measure the distance to the Moon with greater precision. They also deployed a device for monitoring seismic activity and collected some 48 pounds of rocks and dust for scientists to study.

Back aboard *Eagle*, Armstrong and Aldrin rested, then blasted off to their rendezvous with Collins. The three men cheered jubilantly and were "all smiles and giggles," Collins said later. With five months to spare, the late President Kennedy's challenge to put a man on the Moon had been met in a near-perfect mission.

# Aftermath

NASA launched six more Apollo missions to the Moon; the last was in December 1972. Altogether, 12 men walked on the Moon, and did so for increasingly longer periods of time as engineers built upon earlier successes. Astronauts of the last three missions traveled the Moon's surface in a four-wheel drive Lunar Roving Vehicle, which extended the amount of territory they could explore.

The program had a near-disaster with Apollo 13 in April 1970. Halfway to the Moon, an explosion drastically cut the vessel's air, water, and power supplies. Over the next 95 tense hours, the astronauts circled the Moon and flew back to Earth and a safe splashdown. NASA called it "the most successful failure in the annals of space flight."

# PEACE SYMBOL

While the American public passionately debated the nation's role in the Vietnam War in the 1960s, there was no clearer way for an American to telegraph his or her position than to pin on a lapel button emblazoned with the peace symbol. A circle enclosing an upside down Y with a line down the center, the symbol reportedly originated in England, where champions of nuclear disarmament used it in protest marches. Across the Atlantic, it became a ubiquitous shorthand of identity—appearing on banners and posters at antiwar demonstrations, painted on cars, stenciled on sidewalks and walls, used as a motif in jewelry and clothing.

In those tumultuous times, few people had neutral feelings about the peace symbol. In the eyes of the war's most ardent supporters, it was the dishonorable badge of traitors whom they contemptuously referred to as "peaceniks"—a label that smacked of un-American, even Communist sympathies.

Fighting communism had been the U.S. government's rationale for taking sides in the struggle between Communist North Vietnam and the American-supported South. In 1954 President Dwight Eisenhower described the disaster that he believed would spread among Asian nations if South Vietnam fell to the Communists: "You have a row of dominoes set up. You knock over the first one, and what will happen to the last one is a certainty that it will go over very quickly. So you could have a beginning of a disintegration that would have the most profound consequences." To contain the perceived Red menace, the U.S. shored up the South Vietnamese government and army with military advisers, money and matériel.

For close to a decade, most Americans paid scant attention to what was happening in the small, far-away country. But as the conflict dragged on, a growing contingent of critics uneasy about the U.S.

**First used in England, the peace symbol became the emblem of a generation of Americans opposed to the war in Vietnam.**

role began speaking out. Some questioned the strategic importance that President Eisenhower and his advisers ascribed to Vietnam, while others declared that the conflict was a civil war; as they saw it, the U.S. was meddling in another nation's internal affairs. Pacifists were also part of the antiwar vanguard, and in 1963 they organized one of the first major peace demonstrations in New York.

These stirrings of dissent swelled to a clamor after President Lyndon Johnson ordered American ground troops to Vietnam in March 1965. Only months before, during the presidential campaign, Johnson had said that he had no intentions of "committing a good many American boys to fighting a war that I think ought to be fought by the boys of Asia." Remembering those words, thousands of Americans felt angry and betrayed. The White House was picketed, hundreds of small protests erupted all over the country, and on campuses from

Boston to Ann Arbor to Berkeley, students and teachers flocked to "teach-ins" to discuss the war.

Agitation on college campuses spiraled as more and more young men between 18 and 26 were drafted; by 1968, 536,000 Americans were serving in Vietnam. Unlike their poor or working-class contemporaries, college students enjoyed the advantage of a draft deferment. Nevertheless, students defiantly expressed their opposition to the war by burning their draft cards at demonstrations. And, over time, an estimated 80,000 to 100,000 draft resisters fled to Canada and other countries to avoid what one resister described as killing people "for no good reason." Nor were the young alone in decrying the draft. Many well-respected middle-class adults supported them, including the prominent pediatrician Benjamin Spock, who was the co-chairman of the antiwar National Committee for a Sane Nuclear Policy.

"The United States had invaded a country 10,000 miles away with which we had no quarrel. We were killing their people at an alarming rate."

—*David McReynolds, pacifist, 1992*

Mass demonstrations against the war took place in major cities across the nation, including Washington, D.C. (left), where protesters marched outside the Pentagon (right and above).

In 1968 he was convicted of conspiring to counsel draft resisters and sentenced to prison (his conviction was later reversed). Also in '68, two brothers who were Catholic priests, Philip and Daniel Berrigan, led seven other activists in a raid on the draft board of Catonsville, Maryland. They seized the files of more than 300 men who were soon to be drafted and burned them in the parking lot outside as cameras recorded their civil disobedience. Inspired by the Berrigans, other activists carried out similar raids.

Another towering figure in the movement was Nobel Peace laureate Martin Luther King Jr. Although disturbed by the disproportionate number of soldiers who were poor, black and working class, King was reluctant to break with President Johnson because Johnson vigorously supported civil rights. But one day in 1967, after King happened to see a magazine article with color photographs of Viet-

namese children who had been horribly burned by napalm firebombs, he became a committed opponent of the war. He decried the fact that black soldiers were dying "to guarantee liberties in Southeast Asia which they had not found in Southwest Georgia and East Harlem," and he called the U.S. government "the greatest purveyor of violence in the world today."

Peace activists kept up the pressure on the government—marching, fasting, picketing, praying, staging strikes and lobbying. In 1973, the war-weary U.S. finally brought the troops home after signing a treaty with North Vietnam.

# Aftermath

After the U.S. and North Vietnam signed a peace treaty on January 27, 1973, and American troops were withdrawn, antiwar activists lobbied Congress to cut off entirely the military aid still flowing to South Vietnam. In 1974 and 1975, on the anniversaries of the treaty's signing, a coalition of peace groups sponsored rallies and vigils around the nation to remind the American public that North and South Vietnam were still locked in combat. In the spring of '75, after two decades of fighting, the war ended in victory for the North.

# STAR TREK™

With the United States and the Soviet Union launching satellites and men into orbit and toward the Moon, the 1960s must have seemed the perfect time for science fiction to go mainstream. Unfortunately for a television producer and writer named Gene Roddenberry, not all of the television studios thought so. Roddenberry had written for such shows as *Dragnet* and *Have Gun, Will Travel*, but as a lifelong fan of science fiction, he wanted to try his hand at the genre. In a science fiction show, he reasoned, "perhaps I'd be able to talk about love, war, nature, God, sex … and maybe the TV censors would let it pass because it all seemed so make-believe." Inspired by Arthur C. Clarke's nonfiction book, *Profiles of the Future*, Roddenberry crystallized the concept he would pitch to MGM as "Wagon Train to the Stars." MGM and several other studios would pass, but Desilu signed Roddenberry and his show, which, after a few alterations, became *STAR TREK*.

The studios' reluctance notwithstanding, science fiction had already found a niche on television. Series like *Captain Video* and *Buck Rogers* entertained the younger set in the late '40s and '50s, and the dramas *Voyage to the Bottom of the Sea* and *Lost in Space* were popular offerings in the mid-'60s. By September 8, 1966, when NBC launched the *U.S.S. Enterprise*™ on its mission "to boldly go where no man has gone before,"™ the *STAR TREK* universe had developed into a uniquely compelling and serious-minded take on the genre. It didn't hurt, of course, that such notable science fiction writers as Harlan Ellison and Theodore Sturgeon contributed thoughtful scripts, in which good fiction was valued even more than good science.

Set in the twenty-third century, *STAR TREK* presented a reassuring vision of the future to a world caught in the grips of the Cold War. Technology, for example, tended to play a positive role in the

**Beloved *STAR TREK* characters included Kirk, McCoy and Spock (opposite, left to right) and Mr. Scott, the ship's engineer (above).**

# STAR TREK ™

The high-tech *Enterprise* (right) included a transporter that allowed crew members to be "beamed up" to the ship (opposite); the crew was multiethnic, including Uhura from Africa (above left), Asian crewman Sulu and Chekov from Russia (above right, left and right, respectively).

"All I ask is a tall ship, and a star to steer her by. You could feel the wind at your back in those days, the sounds of the sea beneath you and even if you take away the wind and the water, it's still the same. The ship is yours, you can feel her. And the stars are still there...." —*CAPTAIN JAMES T. KIRK*

universe, producing warp engines and miraculous medicines rather than, say, more advanced nuclear weaponry. After all, who would need such weapons in a future in which not just world peace, but also galaxy-wide harmony had been secured under the United Federation of Planets? The crew of the *Enterprise* did frequently contend with Klingons and Romulans, two alien and warlike species that did not belong to the Federation, but it often solved conflicts not in battle but through the astute diplomacy of Captain James T. Kirk™, played by William Shatner. Otherwise the *Enterprise* pursued its essentially humanistic mission to explore the "Final Frontier."

The STAR TREK version of the twenty-third century, of course, often related directly to the social issues folks grappled with in the twentieth-century United States. For example, "Let That Be Your Last Battlefield", in which the *Enterprise* encounters an alien race whose members are irreconcilably split between those with black skin on their right sides and white skin on their left and those whose coloring is reversed, transparently addressed contemporary race relations. In fact, the diversity of the crew, which included the African—and female—Lieutenant Uhura™ (Nichelle Nichols) and Asian helmsman Mr. Sulu™ (George Takei), stemmed from the network and Roddenberry's desire to incorporate more non-white faces in the casts of its shows. "I think it was Gene's vision to have the makeup of the crew reflect the pluralism of this global society," said Takei. "I think Gene has often said, '*The Starship Enterprise*' was the Starship Earth in micro-

STAR TREK brought a variety of vivid characters to the screen, including Ruk (struggling with Kirk at right and played by Ted Cassidy), a race of half-black, half-white beings (inset), and in one episode, the Greek god Apollo (op-

posite); STAR TREK's influence extended to the Jet Propulsion Lab, where scientists wore Spock ears while monitoring *Mariner V* in 1967 (opposite, inset).

cosm.'" The presence of the half-human, half-Vulcan Mr. Spock™ (Leonard Nimoy) among the crew of the *Enterprise* indeed represented the potential for cooperation not just among races, but among species.

Concerned about viewers who might interpret Mr. Spock's features as satanic, NBC airbrushed his arched eyebrows and pointed ears out of early publicity stills. Perhaps the most beloved of the characters whose relationships impelled fans' devotion to the show, Spock and his Vulcan logic served as a foil to Captain Kirk's impetuousness. "Fascinating," Spock would pronounce coolly in the midst of the ship's most bizzare alien encounters, arching one eyebrow even higher with detached curiosity. Dr. Leonard "Bones" McCoy™ (DeForest Kelley), the ship's medical officer, served as Kirk's confidante while his sarcastic humor often placed him at odds with Spock. Finally, when all else failed there was the ship's engineer Mr. Scott (James Doohan) at the ready to use his technical wizardry to save the day.

While the show quickly earned a devoted following, its low ranking among all series caused NBC to decide to cancel it after the second season. A fervent

# Aftermath

STAR TREK fandom, nurtured by "Trekker" fan clubs and conventions, took hold in the '70s when the program went into reruns. In 1979 original cast members were reunited for STAR TREK: *The Motion Picture*™. The movie was a box-office success, and led to the critically acclaimed STAR TREK *II: The Wrath of Khan*™ (1982) which proved the potential of the movie series, now extended to nine films.

In 1987 STAR TREK returned to TV with a new crew in *The Next Generation.* Two more spinoffs, STAR TREK: *Deep Space Nine*™ and STAR TREK: *Voyager*™ debuted in the '90s.

letter-writing campaign sent enough fan mail to NBC offices to convince its executives to keep the show going, however, and although its ratings never improved, STAR TREK endured for one more season, producing 79 episodes—enough for the series to be syndicated and for it to (as the Vulcan saying goes) "live long and prosper" in popular culture.

# GREEN BAY PACKERS

"Winning isn't everything, it's the only thing." For years this quote has been attributed to Vince Lombardi, the dynamic head coach of the Green Bay Packers. In fact, these words were first spoken by John Wayne in the 1953 football film *Trouble Along the Way*. While no one would mistake Lombardi for The Duke, he did command a similar brand of respect among his peers and players. When he spoke, the Packers listened, followed his orders and learned how to win.

After finishing the 1958 season a dismal 1-10-1, the Packers hired the relatively unknown Lombardi, who came to Green Bay with no head coaching experience in college or the pros but an impressive football background nonetheless. In college, Lombardi had been a member of Fordham's famed Seven Blocks of Granite offensive line, and as an assistant at Army he had worked alongside passing

guru and future Hall-of-Fame coach Sid Gillman. When the Packers called, the 45-year-old Lombardi was the offensive coordinator for the New York Giants.

It took Lombardi one season to turn the Pack around. Passionately demanding, he expected each player to execute his assigned task flawlessly; to achieve this he made them learn and practice each play over and over. Defensive tackle Henry Jordan described Lombardi's approach this way: "He treated us all the same, like dogs."

With 14 returning starters from the previous year, the Packers finished a respectable 7–5 in 1959. The following year they won the NFL's Western Conference with an 8–4 record and went on to face the Philadelphia Eagles in the championship game. The Packers lost 17–13 as fullback Jim Taylor was stopped on the Eagles' eight-yard

**The perfectionist Lombardi (left) and the professional Starr (above, No. 15) led the Packers to five NFL titles in the '60s.**

line on the game's final play. This would be the last championship game Lombardi's Packers would ever lose.

Entering the 1960 season, the newly confident Packers had a formidable team. Four-year veteran quarterback Bart Starr was joined in the backfield by the dangerous duo of punishing fullback Taylor and multitalented halfback Paul Hornung, who not only ran, caught and passed the ball but kicked field goals and extra points as well. Protecting Starr and company were fearsome offensive linemen such as tackle Forrest Gregg and guards Jerry Kramer and Fred (Fuzzy) Thurston. The defense was anchored by menacing middle linebacker Ray Nitschke and agile defensive back Herb Adderley. But this was by no means a team dominated by stars; the Packers were rather a product of Lombardi's philosophy that every single starter and backup had a role to play and needed to execute that role to perfec-

The versatile Hornung (left, above) could run, pass, catch, punt or kick the ball; the Green Bay defense (above) was a fe- rocious bunch, led by future Hall of Famer Ray Nitschke (No. 66), one of the most fearsome middle linebackers in NFL history.

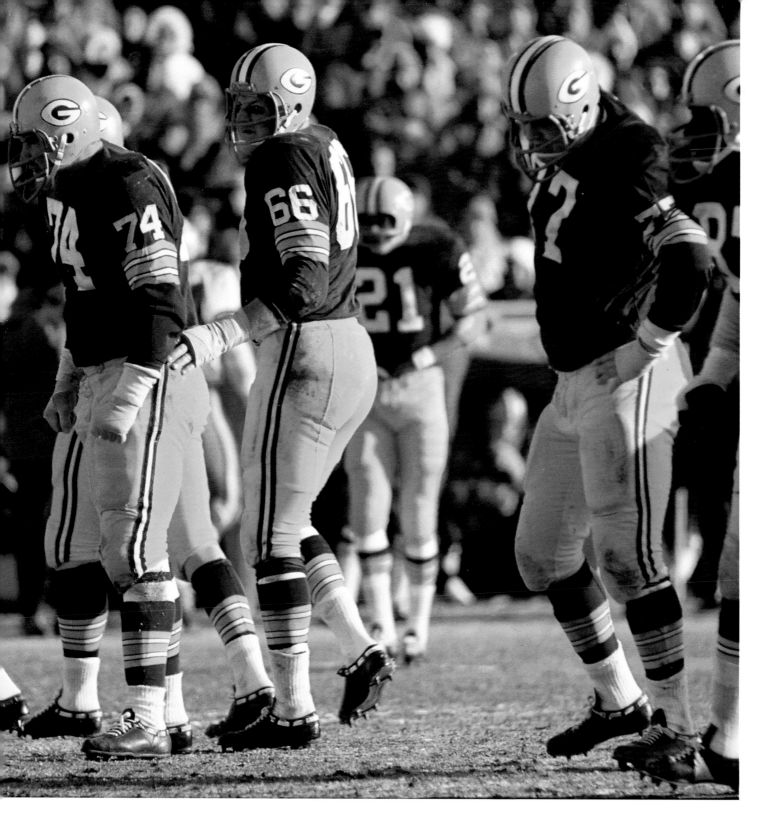

"You might reduce Lombardi's coaching philosophy to a single sentence: In any game, you do the things you do best and you do them over and over and over."

—*GEORGE HALAS, coach and owner, Chicago Bears*

tion for the team to succeed. And succeed it did.

In 1961 the Packers won the NFL championship with a 37–0 drubbing of the New York Giants. It was Green Bay's first NFL title in 17 years. The Packers beat the Giants again in the 1962 title game, 16–7, as Jim Taylor tied an NFL playoff record with 31 carries (for 85 yards) and scored Green Bay's lone touchdown. Their next NFL title came following the 1965 season as they defeated the Cleveland Browns 23–12 in the championship game.

Green Bay returned to the NFL title game the following year and beat the Dallas Cowboys 34–27. That season, however, would include one more critical game that put the prestige of the NFL on the line against the upstart American Football League. Led by game MVP Starr, Green Bay rolled to an easy 35–10 win over the Kansas City Chiefs in the inaugural Super Bowl (*see page 23*).

After the next season, on December 31, 1967, the Packers played the Cowboys on Green Bay's Lambeau Field for the NFL title in what became a landmark game in the Pack's storied history. The temperature was -13°, with a cutting 15-mile-per-hour wind—brutal conditions that gave rise to the epic contest's legendary moniker, "The Ice Bowl." Trailing 17–14, the Packers had the ball at their own 32-yard line with 4:50 left. Mixing its power running game with short passes from Starr, Green Bay methodically moved downfield. Just inside Dallas's one-yard line with 16 seconds left, the Packers called time out. Lombardi decided to eschew a tying field goal attempt when Starr convinced his coach that he could score on a quarterback sneak. On a frozen field, with unsure footing, Starr lowered his head and plunged into the end zone behind Kramer to give the Packers a thrilling 21–17 victory and a third straight NFL title.

The Packers went on to wallop Oakland 33–14 in Super Bowl II, a victory that convinced Lombardi it was time to retire. During its decade of dominance Green Bay won five NFL titles and ran away with the first two Super Bowls. For Lombardi's Packers, winning *was* the only thing.

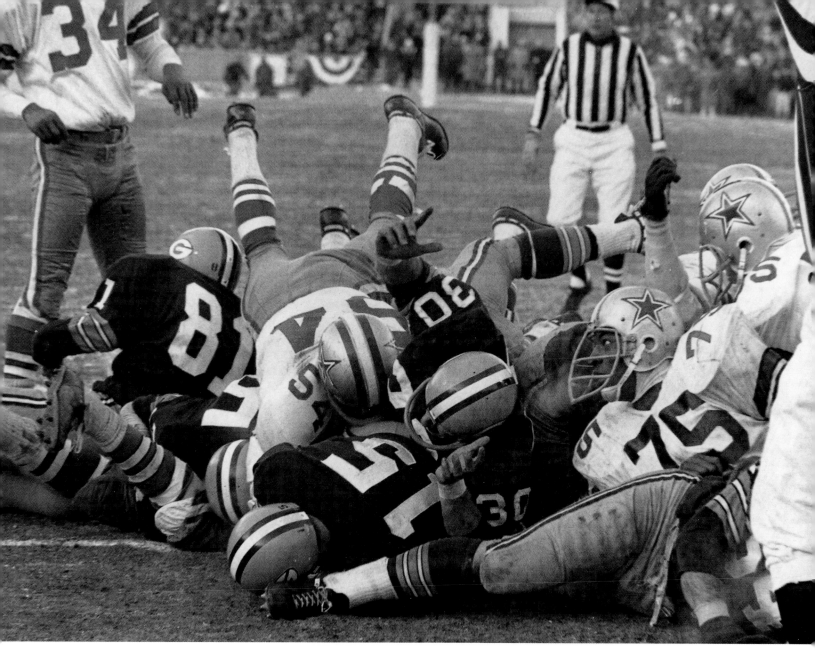

# Aftermath

When Starr (15) dived across the goal line with the winning score in the Ice Bowl (above), he capped one of the Packers' most dramatic victories; to their opponents in the first two Super Bowls, the real Packers must have seemed almost as big as their simulated selves (opposite page).

In the '70s and '80s the Packers went through a succession of lean years and coaches, including former greats Bart Starr and Forrest Gregg. Green Bay's fortunes changed in 1992 when the team hired San Francisco 49ers offensive coordinator Mike Holmgren as head coach and traded for quarterback Brett Favre from the Atlanta Falcons. When perennial All-Pro defensive end Reggie White was signed in 1993, the Pack, it appeared, was back.

During the next few years Favre flourished under Holmgren's tutelage and new offense, and White continued to terrorize opposing quarterbacks. On January 26, 1997, the Packers won their first NFL title in 29 years, defeating the New England Patriots 35–21 in Super Bowl XXXI.

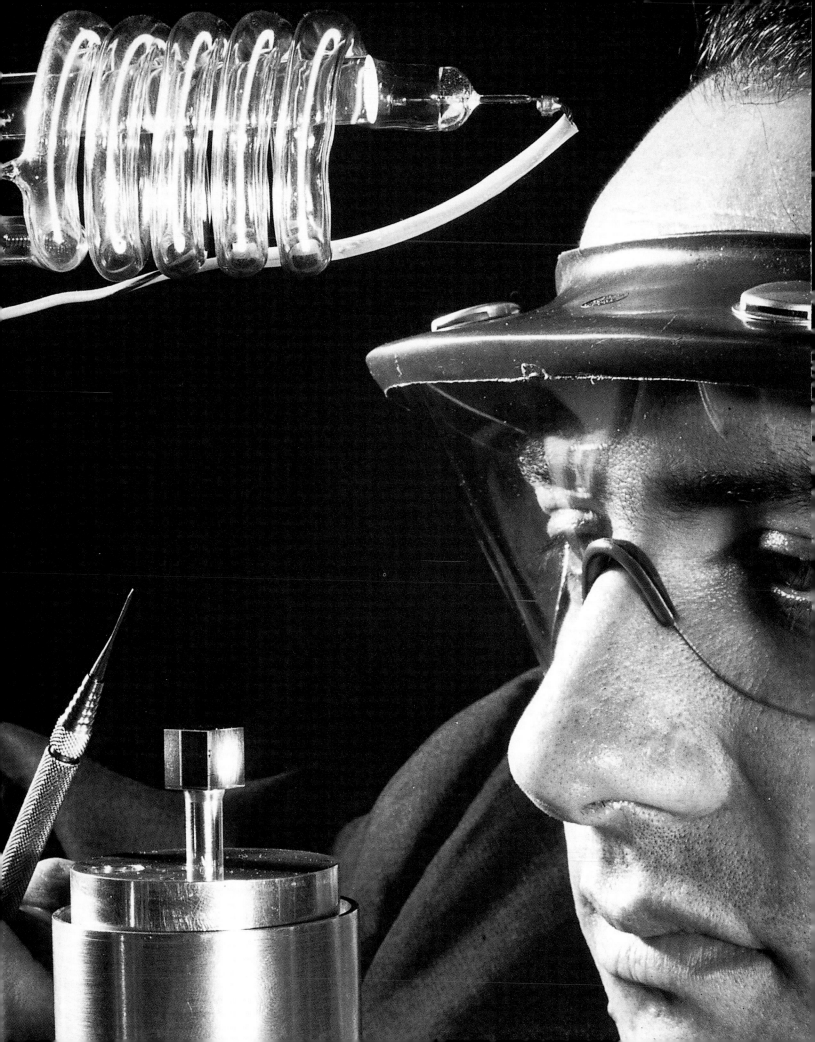

# LASERS

"Suddenly there was a flash of light. It was sweeping round swiftly and steadily, this flaming death, this invisible, inevitable sword of heat," wrote H. G. Wells in his 1898 novel, *The War of the Worlds*. Subsequent works of science fiction filled Americans' imaginations with similar visions of ray guns that could destroy entire cities with a single beam of intense, focused energy. The first actual lasers, however, were much tamer machines than their terrifying fictional counterparts. A narrow cylinder of ruby about one inch long and enclosed within the coil of a flash lamp, the first laser was in fact so small you could rest it in the palm of your hand.

An acronym for "light amplification by stimulated emission of radiation," the word *laser* refers not as much to a device as it does to the process that produces an extremely focused beam of electromagnetic radiation. Albert Einstein first proposed the theory of stimulated emission in 1916. He observed that radiation—light, for example—at a particular wavelength should stimulate an excited electron to emit radiation at the same wavelength. In an environment where most electrons are excited, these waves of radiation can set off a chain reaction that results in a burst of radiation energy at a single wavelength; collected with mirrors, that burst can be focused into an intense beam of energy.

A significant barrier stood between Einstein's theory and the first laser, however, for physicists could not imagine how to create or maintain an environment in which more electrons are excited than not. Not until 1951 did Charles Townes, a physics professor at Columbia University, con-

**The elegant ruby laser of Theodore Maiman (left) evolved into more sophisticated versions (above).**

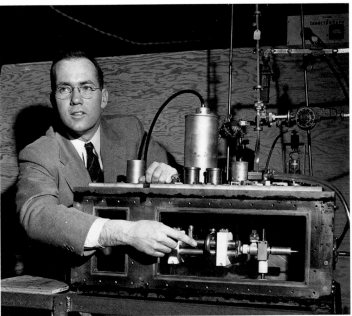

A maser, the predecessor to the laser, was used by Townes to power an "atomic clock" (above); Dr. A. Stevens Halsted demonstrated a continuous-wave argon ion laser (left); lasers were eventually used to create holograms (opposite, left) and in more fanciful settings such as the James Bond movie, *Goldfinger* (opposite, inset).

ceive of the system that could produce an intense beam of microwave radiation by stimulated emission. Nearly three years later he and his associates at Columbia made what he called a "maser"— the *m* standing for the microwaves produced by the device.

While it turned out to have only a limited range of applications, the maser represented a significant breakthrough on the way to assembling the first lasers, and in 1964 Townes shared the Nobel Prize in physics with two Soviet scientists, Nikolai Basov and Alexander Prokhorov, for their contributions to the development of laser technology. Lasers work in essentially the same way as masers, but they emit visible light and other forms of radiation at higher energy levels and frequencies.

In December 1958 Townes and his colleague Arthur Schawlow, who had worked as a postdoctoral fellow under Townes before he took a job with Bell Laboratories in 1951, published "Infrared and Optical Masers," a paper that mapped out the theoretical groundwork for laser development and set scientists scrambling to be the first to build the device. Only a year and a half later Theodore Maiman, a physicist at Hughes Research Laboratories in Malibu, California, won the race with his elegant miniature ruby laser. He first demonstrated the effectiveness of the device on May 16, 1960, and the July 7 announcement of his success took the scientific community by surprise, for in 1959 Schawlow had pronounced ruby unsuitable for producing a laser beam.

"At the time, a colleague described the laser as a solution looking for a problem," Townes said later. Nevertheless, an endless array of problems—medical, industrial, scientific and military—would soon invite solutions by laser applications, and

within the decade lasers proliferated, using a wide variety of materials—gases, liquids, crystals and other solids—to produce radiation at a variety of wavelengths. Much of the research that produced these lasers was conducted in the laboratories of corporations such as Bell, which hoped to discover communications applications for the devices. In the '80s this research resulted in the fiberoptic communications revolution. Other applications were discovered more quickly. For example, because a laser beam does not diffuse like a beam of ordinary light, scientists could pinpoint one on a mirror placed on the Moon by Apollo 11 astronauts and use it to measure the distance between the Moon and the Earth with precision.

While the military found immediate uses for distance-measuring lasers, producing anything like a ray gun proved far more complicated. But in the late '60s a team of scientists at Berkeley that included Townes discovered a maser emanating from the gases of outer space. It was not, alas, the "invisible, inevitable sword of heat" of an approaching Martian army, but a naturally occurring phenomenon.

# Aftermath

Now, of course, lasers do their work everywhere, including in the scanners at your local supermarket, the printer at your office and the CD player in your living room. The military uses lasers in its missile guidance systems; industry uses lasers to weld and to cut metals and plastics; and science uses lasers to probe and measure otherwise out-of-reach locations. And lasers now provide everyday miracles as they save eyesight and lives, having replaced the scalpel in some surgeries and made others—such as the correction of a detached retina—much more practicable.

# INDEX